PSYCHOLOGY FOR
TEACHING ASSISTANTS

PSYCHOLOGY FOR TEACHING ASSISTANTS

*Christopher Arnold and
Jane Yeomans*

Trentham Books

Stoke on Trent, UK and Sterling, USA

Trentham Books Limited

Westview House	22883 Quicksilver Drive
734 London Road	Sterling
Oakhill	VA 20166-2012
Stoke on Trent	USA
Staffordshire	
England ST4 5NP	

First published 2005

British Library Cataloguing-in-Publication Data
A catalogue record for this book is available from the British Library

ISBN-13: 978-1-85856-309-1
ISBN-10: 1-85856-309-7

Designed and typeset by Trentham Print Design Ltd., Chester and printed in Great Britain by Cromwell Press Ltd., Wiltshire.

Contents

Acknowledgments

The authors are extremely grateful to friends and colleagues at Sandwell's Inclusion Support Service under the leadership of Pat Evans for their advice and support. Thanks are also due to the administrative staff based at 12 Grange Road and Connor Education Centre for their patience and assistance and to Maggie Ray Jones for her assistance with the final version of the book. Particular thanks go to Paula Carbini, Ardenio Ottaviani, Gemma Winter and Sylvia Arnold for their assistance with part 5 of this book. Finally. we thank Gillian Klein for her patience and faith.

Dedication: To our families

Part 1
Introduction and Context

1

Introduction to Theories

This chapter

- ■ introduces the concepts of *schools of psychology* and *range of convenience* of theories

- ■ describes the leading schools of psychology

- ■ outlines the ranges of convenience of the different schools

Why study psychology? If psychology is the science of mental life (Miller) and education is a system of practical arrangements made for children to promote their intellectual, social, emotional and moral development (Reeve) then psychology is an obvious way of developing the education of young people. It provides:

- ■ ways of thinking about and understanding children

- ■ ways of getting information about children's learning

- ■ a vast, world wide source of information about different people collected in a systematic way

Psychology is often described as a young science. It is certainly true that, as a separate university discipline, it has been in existence for much less time than physics, maths or medicine, but it has evolved from a wide variety of sources and has developed to a position from which many people may say that they are 'psychologists', but do very different kinds of work. In addition, there are many different kinds of psychology. The groups are sometimes called schools.

We emphasise the term *different* as it is worth understanding the different ways in which different schools of psychology think. Different schools have different assumptions about people and the way they work. Perhaps confusingly, different schools can reach different conclusions about the problems they work on. However these different schools survive because they help illuminate different human problems. Each school uses different theories which work in different ways for different problems. The extent that a particular theory is useful is sometimes called the Range of Convenience of the theory.

In this book, we represent different schools of psychology to see how they apply to children and the ways in which their education can be enhanced by teaching assistants. Sometimes the different theories appear to contradict themselves, but by understanding the differences we will make sense of the whole picture.

Biological psychology

A number of areas which are relevant to our work come into this school. We shall consider child development and the biological basis for behaviour.

We are all born into our worlds in bodies which are constructed in particular ways. There are differences between us which are controlled by biological differences. People grow at different rates: hair colour, eye colour, right and left handedness are all controlled by our biological make-up. Biologists recognise the importance of children's environments in shaping their development in the context of different genes and individual biological differences. We begin with child development.

Developmental psychology

Developmental psychologists are interested in discovering information about how the brain grows, the influence that the child's environment has on it and in discovering ways to avoid difficulties for children. They have considered the stages of development and the question of critical periods in child development.

In the development of walking in infants there is a clear sequence which could be characterised as:

1. rolling over
2. bearing some weight on legs
3. sitting without support
4. standing, holding furniture
5. crawling
6. walking, holding furniture
7. standing alone
8. walking alone

This sequence illustrates three different elements of considering the development of walking as going through different stages.

1. behaviours at each stage have a particular theme
2. behaviours at each stage are different from those in different stages
3. children go through each stage in the same order

Although this is a seemingly obvious way of looking at walking, not all psychologists agree about the usefulness of thinking about stages. It might be more useful to consider development as a continuous process. More recently, however, developmental psychologists have been able to look at developmental transitions and have started to see the value of examining developmental stages.

A particularly well-known developmental sequence is that described by Jean Piaget which will be described in the cognitive psychology section of this chapter.

Many other areas of child development have been described in terms of stages. Language, moral development, problem solving and friendships have all been studied and stages suggested. Some of these are examined in the main body of the book, but the existence of *critical periods* is important to outline at this point.

If young children have very different experiences from those of the majority of the population, do those experiences have lasting and irreversible effects on their adult lives? Suggestions that this might be true came from observations of children in orphanages and long-stay isolation hospitals. A paediatrician called Rutter noticed that children were more likely to have difficulties sustaining long-term adult relationships if they were from this group. However, when children in orphanages and in long-term isolation hospitals were given an adult figure, who formed an attachment with them, the outcome was more positive. This work was explored further with animals raised with and without parents. Those animals raised in isolation were less likely to sustain families than those raised more conventionally. This led to the concept of a critical period in children's lives. If certain factors such as attachment to an adult are not available, then long-term and irreversible effects can occur.

Recent work suggests that for development of walking, there are no critical periods. Children who are unable to crawl can catch up, given the appropriate help. Critical periods in the emotional development of children are still considered useful concepts. There are initiatives to provide different educational experiences for children who have not been securely attached to parents. One example of this is the development of nurture groups in schools. These use higher adult to pupil ratios and broaden the type of activities undertaken to include meal times..

Question: To what extent do you think that the way you behave and think is a reflection of the relationships you had in early childhood?

Biological bases for behaviour

Biologists often analyse human behaviour in two different ways – the *cause* of behaviour and the *function* of behaviour. Workers looking at *causes* of human behaviour may look at how the brain is functioning and the chemical and electrical activities found there. Those looking at *function* examine why a particular human activity is useful to the individual and therefore why it is maintained. The example of alcohol addiction highlights the differences.

Until the beginning of the last century, people who drank a lot of alcohol were considered to be weak and have deficiencies in their character. Well-meaning philanthropists would attempt to assist. Not many people know that Yate's Wine Lodges were started by Peter Yate as a way of decreasing people's gin drinking. It was considered better that they drank the less strong, and morally favourable, wine. Biological psychologists study the effect that alcohol has on the brain. There are numerous ways in which the chemistry of the brain is affected. Alcohol is a powerful solvent. The ways in which our brains work is affected by alcohol. Our moods change and we can feel more optimistic, less anxious. Experiments with rats and humans show that there are differences in the ways that brains respond to alcohol. This leads to the conclusion that differences in the consumption of alcohol may be a result of the differences in our brain chemistry. Alcoholism can run in families and rats can be selectively bred to increase their use of alcohol. All this suggests a genetic, and therefore biological, cause for alcoholism. Alcoholics are not alcoholics because they are weak but because their brains work differently from other people's. In the same way that some people are more prone to illness than others, some people are more prone to alcoholism than others. This leads us to think of alcoholism as a *disease* which *causes* drinking rather than as a sign of personal weakness.

The *functional* analysis takes a rather different view. Any behaviour which continues over time only does so because it fulfils a need in the person. In other words its *function* is to meet a need. Two psychologists called Cox and Klinger suggested that the decision to drink alcohol is based on whether the benefits outweigh the drawbacks. They describe the expectation that people drink because they expect a more satisfying mental state after they have taken the drink than before. People might drink because they are bored and want to achieve something in their public or private world. There is a discrepancy between the individual's actual view of themselves and their ideal view of themselves. This view is supported by another psychologist, Alexander, who sees alcoholism as an adaptation to a situation which might create depression or social isolation. If life holds no hope of development and growth, alcoholism is a real, and more stimulating option. People drink to excess because it is better than the alternative. This view can also be applied to the widespread use of an anti-depressant called Valium, in the 1970s.

At that time there was a tendency to build tall tower blocks of flats which were used by councils to house people with low incomes. The theory was that the amount of land freed up would encourage communal living and generate new societies. In fact many of the inhabitants were young mothers who felt trapped in their new homes. They became depressed: they had little money and were looking after young children, often on their own. They went to their doctors, who, recognising their depression, prescribed Valium. Many became addicted to the drug.

Question: Was the Valium addiction a result of a disease or an adaption to an unsatisfactory environment?

The biological perspective can be taken a lot further. In particular, it can be taken to areas of human behaviour and thoughts. If human behaviour has any kind of genetic component the work of Charles Darwin is relevant. The scientist, Richard Dawkins, modified Darwin's reasoning to cover behaviour. The argument is this. If a particular human behaviour has a genetic component and genes are passed on to children then human behaviour is more likely to be successful if it is more likely to promote itself through transmission of the genes to children. Dawkins is simply stating that the genes most likely to survive to the next generation are likely to be selected and to thrive in the long term. Behaviour with a genetic component is likely to promote the genes which influence that behaviour. Through this process the behaviour is likely to be promoted too.

This way of thinking has often been applied to differences in sexual behaviour between men and women. For a woman's genes to be promoted through her children, there needs to be a successful child. For a woman to have a successful child requires a considerable investment of time. Apart from the pregnancy and birth, the child will probably be dependent on the mother's care for a considerable number of years. The mother, in turn, may be dependent on support for much of that time. Accordingly, it is in the mother's interests to choose a partner who is likely to be loyal over time. Whereas, for a man, the investment can be very short. Until very recently, it was impossible for a man to be completely sure that a child was genetically his. It is more advantageous for a man to have multiple partners, in the hope that his genes will spread to the next generation.

These ideas are contentious and may even appear a little far fetched. However there is some experimental support for them. The psychologists, Buss and others, asked men and women to imagine their partners having intercourse with someone else, or forming a deep emotional attachment to another person. In addition to the answers, the subjects were attached to a machine which measures the electrical conductivity of the skin. This technique has been used to measure emotional arousal. As predicted by the theory, more women than men were made anxious by the thought of deep emotional attachment, and more men than women were made anxious by the thought of sexual intercourse. The theory explains this because the woman becomes anxious that the man may no longer support her child (and therefore her genes) and the man becomes anxious that a child born to his partner may not have his genes.

The theory highlights the interaction between biology and environment. The last example is based on the work of Friedman and Rosenman, first published in the 1970s. They were researching factors which contributed to heart attacks and identified two different types of responses to stressful situations. One group of people got more and more stressed whilst the other group did not. The group which got more stressed was generally highly competitive and achievement oriented. In traffic jams members of this group got more impatient and angry. They were called Type A. Later work suggested that anger and aggression were good predictors of heart attack susceptibility. The other group responded more calmly and accepted the inevitable outcome. They were called Type B. Type A people were more likely to have heart attacks. The mechanism by which getting stressed leads to physiological changes which may lead to heart attacks is quite well understood. So is the link between personality type and heart attacks inevitable? Not necessarily. It is possible to teach a Type A person how to respond more like a Type B person.

The features of Type A behaviour are:

■ thinking of or doing two things at once

■ planning more and more activities into less and less time

■ failing to notice or be interested in the environment

■ hurrying the speech of others

■ becoming unduly irritated when forced to wait in a queue or when following a car travelling more slowly than you would like

■ believing that if you want something done well you have to do it yourself

■ frequent knee jiggling or rapid finger tapping

■ being obsessed about being on time

■ playing nearly every game to win (even with children)

■ becoming impatient while watching others do things you think you can do better or faster

Question: To what extent do you see those features as being changeable in people?

The biological approach to psychology is good at recognising the importance of the genetic predispositions to certain courses of action. Later it will be shown that it accounts well for the different approaches to anger in children. It offers insights into the ways in which both younger children and teenagers interact in schools. It provides good accounts for the kinds of differences that are found in children who abuse drugs. It is less convincing in accounting for the ways in which children learn. This is better explained by behavioural psychology.

Behavioural psychology

Learning is a central part of our existence. For behavioural psychologists, there is a simple assumption that learning is best understood in terms which are external to the human body. Watch what people *do* rather than what they *say* they do or think. Additionally, there is an assumption that laws of learning apply for all species. Finally, learning complex things is dependent on learning simple things first. So, we can study learning by looking at the behaviours of other animals. Rats, pigeons, chickens, beetles and chimpanzees can all help in the understanding of human development and learning. There are two fundamental methods of learning known as *classical* and *operant*.

Classical conditioning was first described by the Russian scientist Pavlov who was researching how the digestive system worked. He used dogs to find a way of measuring the saliva produced by the dog when presented with food. To his surprise, he found that after a short time, the dogs would produce saliva before the food was presented. He assumed that the dogs were salivating when they heard the person approach with the food. When he investigated further, he found that he was able to teach a dog to salivate to the sound of a bell, provided the dog had heard the bell around feeding time. The dog had learned to associate the bell with the food, or Pavlov had conditioned the saliva to be produced to the sound of a bell rather than food. He went on further. If the conditioned dog heard the bell and did not receive food, eventually the dog stopped salivating to the sound of the bell. This analysis can be applied to children in a very wide range of circumstances. Newly-born children will turn their mouths towards most objects which touch their faces. They quickly learn to turn only when the object is associated with feeding, such as a nipple or feeding bottle. Children who have had a frightening experience, which they relate with a particular place, can be fearful if they revisit that place, or even one like it. This method of analysis is particularly good when children's responses are more biological in nature, like fear, pleasure and other emotions.

The second type is *operant* conditioning. The psychologist, Skinner, is best known for his work with the behaviour of rats. Rats were placed in specially designed cages in which a lever was available. If the rat pressed the lever, it got a small sugar pellet. Rats like sugar pellets. Once the rat discovered this, it would press again to get more pellets. The experimenters could change the mechanism to vary the relationship between the number of presses and the arrival of the sugar pellet. The rats consistently learned to respond in the same ways. Other experiments used the boxes in less pleasant ways. Rats were given small electric shocks if they performed certain actions. As you might expect, the rats learned to avoid these actions.

The general principles are these:

If an action is followed by a reward, it is more likely to be repeated.
If an action is followed by something unpleasant, it is less likely to be repeated.
Clearly what counts with animals as a reward is based on whether the animal will choose it.

The theory goes further. Once a child has learned to associate a particular action with a reward, they may repeat the action in slightly different circumstances. A child who has been taught to take their dirty shoes off indoors may do the same in another house. This is called *generalisation*. A child may then learn that it is not necessary to take their shoes off when they go into a shop or public building. This learning is called *discrimination*.

The applications of *operant* conditioning in the classroom are numerous. If children associate a reward with a particular action, they are more likely to repeat it. If they associate something unpleasant with a particular action, they are less likely to repeat it. At this point the theory does not consider the use of a reward *before* an action. This is commonly known as a bribe: if I give you a sweet, will you keep quiet for the next five minutes? Bribes do not feature in *operant* conditioning, unless seen from the child's perspective. The child can be said to be conditioning the adult by rewarding them (for example by being quiet for a little time) if the adult gives a sweet. In general, bribing does not work.

Behavioural psychologists are interested in analysing behaviour by looking at the events leading up to an action *classical conditioning* and those following a course of action *operant conditioning*. An easy way to remember this is by thinking about the ABC of behaviour:

Antecedants –	Behaviour	Consequences
Events prior to the behaviour		Events following the behaviour

Question: Can you analyse an element of your behaviour, perhaps an undesirable element, in terms of the Antecedents and Consequences. Which of these could be changed if you wanted to change this aspect of your behaviour?

An alternative to classical and operant conditioning

Behavioural psychology has developed and examined different ways of learning. *Social learning theory* arose from this school and highlights the possibility that we might learn by watching others. The name most associated with this theory is Bandura, who called this type of learning *modelling*. Children who see other children behaving in a certain way are more inclined to copy their actions. A key study in this area involved children watching a video of an adult being violent towards a toy doll. When the children were able to play with the doll themselves, they were much more likely to behave aggressively than if they had not seen the video. The importance of this in the context of schools is clear. If children see adults behaving aggressively towards themselves or others, they are more likely to behave in the same way themselves. This theory provided a sound theoretical basis for banning corporal punishment in schools.

These are the three fundamental types of learning studied by behavioural psychologists. The range of convenience of this school of psychology is vast. It extends far beyond teaching children how to behave in and outside school into teaching individual skills like reading and maths. However, there is a view that to ignore what people *think*, a large source of information about the way people work is lost. Our next school of psychology, *experiential psychology,* starts from that point.

Experiential psychology

Sometimes called *humanistic psychology*, this school starts with the assumption that we all have unique and different experiences which shape our thinking and behaviour and that subjective experience and our awareness of ourselves are legitimate and important phenomena to be studied. Our existences as people are important. The terms *phenomenological* and *existential* approaches to psychology are thus created. Different areas of study are found. To be a person is to experience ourselves living in a world: we have intentions and act on them. Finally we are able to reflect on ourselves and think about what we have done, thought and felt.

Much information about the way we work has arisen from this school, which will be illustrated by looking at the issue of autonomy and determinism. Studies in institutions in which residents are not able to choose elements of their daily lives for themselves are more likely to become depressed and live shorter lives. Residents in environments which encourage participation in decision making are more likely to be happier and live longer. Our experience of being able to choose for ourselves is important. It comes at a price, though. For many, total freedom to decide how we live is frightening. It may be easier to delegate responsibility to some external group, such as society or a moral or religious code, but existentialists argue that this decision is still a matter for the individual. An obvious application of these ideas in the area of supporting children is in the use of choice in the classroom. Much of the experience of school is driven by time-tables and programmes of work. Children can find that they have little choice in what is done in schools. The use of genuine options may help to engage children in their own learning and empower them to become healthy and autonomous adults.

The knowledge that each of us has a unique experience can assist in understanding the positions of others. A mother of a child who had Perthe's disease was distressed when the child became sad because nobody would play with her. The disease affects hip joints and can lead to limited mobility. The mother kept telling the child that the other children weren't really intending to be unkind. In addition, she said that she knew how her daughter felt. The mother was getting more and more distraught and frustrated. She approached the psychologist, who encouraged her to think very differently about her daughter. The mother had never experienced life with Perthe's disease. She didn't know how her daughter felt, nor could she. By changing the script to acknowledge her daughter's distress by saying 'That must make you very sad, is there anything anyone can do to help?' she was able to achieve much more than her previous attempts at comforting.

Within this school we find a study of the search for meaning. Why are we here? What is life for? These questions can be fundamental for us. They are not simply the province of adults. Children can be just as concerned. The quest for meaning can lead to religion, philosophy and a great deal of self-reflection. Some argue that it can lead to madness, but it seems to be a feature of mankind that meaning is essential to *good* mental health. Without it, there can be a great deal of personal *angst*, and even suicide. We should not assume that what is meaningful in our lives will be meaningful for children in theirs. For children in distress the use of non-judgemental counselling is often adopted. This approach has its origins in humanistic psychology. We are each different, with unique experiences and life stories to tell. Experiential psychology focuses on the individual. The school of *social constructionism* starts from the assumption that we are primarily social.

Question: Have there been people you have met who have had very different experiences which influence the way they see the world?

Social constructionism

Mankind has created the most sophisticated societies in the world. The ways in which these societies shape us is the starting point for this school of psychology. The way we think, and therefore behave, is a result of interactions we have had with other people and situations. It may be a little odd to think in these terms, but knowledge is not something either out there to be learned, or something just inside our heads, but something that has been made jointly with other people. This school also examines the ways in which we see ourselves. There is a distinction between *I* and *me*. The *I* in this approach refers to the conscious being that communicates. The *me* refers to the image I have of myself. This image that we have of ourselves is something learned and not there at birth. We learn to see ourselves through the eyes of others. The *me* is the result of my experiences of other people experiencing me. An example will make this clearer.

A child may be told that they are good or bad. If they are told consistently that they are bad they may begin to think that they are bad. The image that the child has of themselves is that they are bad. This can have a profound influence on the way they think and behave. If a child believes that they are bad, an adult who says that they are good or have behaved in a good way may cause that child distress, because they are not confirming the image that the child has of themselves. This may cause the child to behave in a worse way so that the child shows the adult that they are really bad. A child who has been consistently told that they are worthless may believe that they are unlovable. If an adult appears and says that they are good and can be loved, this can cause a problem for the child. The thoughts can go like this:

> I know that I am unlovable.
> This grown up says that I am good and lovable.
> Therefore, either I have got it wrong about myself,
> or this grown up is worthless because they can't see that I am unlovable.
> I couldn't possibly love someone who loves me, because if they love me they are worthless.

This reaction can also lead to children behaving in an even more outrageous way, to prove to the adult that they are as bad they believe themselves to be. This is not to say that there are children who should not receive praise. We are recognising the different effects that praise may have on children.

This school of psychology places a great emphasis on the importance of language. Words do not exist in isolation. They are used by people and can have subtle and sometimes very powerful ways of shaping the way we think. The terms idiot, imbecile, moron, cretin and ineducable would now be considered offensive and unacceptable, but they were quite commonly used by educated people to describe children until surprisingly recently.

A second example can be found in children's knowledge about hitting other children. There are families where children who do not hit back may be called 'sissy'. Children who do hit back are justified. Children who hit others without reason may be described as 'spoiled'. Parents may be concerned that their children are not seen as 'sissy' or 'spoiled'.

Our third example looks at the ways in which we behave differently in different contexts. All of us work and live in different groups of people, be they our own families, in our work places or wen we are with different groups of friends. Social constructionism suggests that our 'selves' can be different in these different places. Although I am the same person in each context, I will think, speak and behave differently in each. We can all think of examples. It is very unlikely that we would use the same language with our parents as with our school friends. Children learn the different roles of being in a class or being in the playground as well as being in their families. It is by recognising that children are constructing different identities that we can help those who have been told that they are bad.

As we can see, the applications of this school to the lives of children are widespread. We should not assume that children's experiences of their social worlds are the same. When children start education, or change area and culture, the possibility of misunderstanding is high. Education can be a unifier and a place in which children learn to communicate, as can other shared experiences such as television or text messaging. Social constructionism helps us to understand the diversity of childrens' experiences and the ways in which this diversity influences how they think and act.

Question: Can you think of groups (or families) who think in very different ways from you?

Cognitive psychology

If we asked members of the public what psychology is about, the chances are that they would associate it with the last two schools described. The term *cognitive* comes from the Latin word for knowledge and is concerned with the study of mental processes of thought and knowledge.

A *cognitive* approach to psychology emphasises the importance of mental activity and mental processes. A cognitive psychologist attributes feelings and behaviour to internal mental states. Many aspects of cognitive psychology that are relevant to the context of school. This section is designed to give an overview of the approach, so will focus on listing and defining some key elements, together with an outline of some of the significant theories that contribute to this approach.

A cognitive approach involves the following key elements:

Memory

Learning and remembering are important aspects of schooling. Memory is generally considered to comprise two elements: short term and long term memory. Information is initially received in the short term memory. Transfer to the long term memory has to take place so that the individual does not forget. This process of transfer will be dealt with in more detail when we look at the processes of learning.

Perception

Human beings gather information through their senses: sight, hearing, smell, touch, taste. Perception is the way in which our brain makes sense of all these sensory messages. We use our previous knowledge and experience in this process.

Attention

You have probably met many children who have 'poor attention'. The ability to focus on a particular stimulus which often means being able to 'tune out' other stimuli around us is the essence of attention. The information received by our senses is part of the process of perception. Attention means that we have to filter out some of this information, in order to concentrate on, or pay attention to, what is important or relevant. Think about the school staff room at break time. Many members of staff will be present, and usually a buzz of conversation. You might be aware that other groups are talking or that the photocopier is whirring away in the corner, but you can filter out these sounds and attend to the conversation you are having with your colleague.

Motivation

Basically, this means how much the individual wants to do something. Motivation is divided into two elements: extrinsic and intrinsic. These can be explained by using examples from everyday life. Think about a hobby or activity that you particularly enjoy. You probably don't need too much persuasion to pursue these activities. You are intrinsically motivated to do them. Now, think about something you don't particularly like doing, and the circumstances in which you would do this activity. It's likely that there is some kind of 'pay off' for doing it. For example, the extrinsic motivation for continuing in a job which is not particularly enjoyable, is likely to be the salary at the end of the month. This is extrinsic motivation.

Concept development

A concept is a mental representation of an object and a means of classifying objects according to common properties. Think about the word 'dog'. What mental picture do you have? Whatever it is, it is likely that your mental picture will have four legs and a tail. You will be able to tell me the common properties of dogs such as barking. If I tell you that a fnarr has four legs, a tail and a very loud bark, you might treat this new piece of information by classifying it as a dog. Children develop concepts through their experience of the world around them. You might have come across young children who over generalise such as a child who calls all four legged animals dog. A more embarrassing example, experienced by a friend, was that of her child calling all men in uniform 'daddy', because his father wore a uniform. These examples are quite normal in a child's development. As children experience more and more examples of objects or people, their concepts are refined and they are more able to process new information.

Intellectual development

This aspect of *cognitive* psychology is related to learning and intelligence. Subsequent chapters will cover these aspects of the cognitive approach in more detail. This section will give you an overview of some of the key contributors in the field of intellectual development.

The work of Jean Piaget

Jean Piaget was a Swiss psychologist who developed his theories during the early part of the twentieth century. The influence of his theory about the intellectual development of children can still be seen in classrooms today.

Piaget suggested that there are four stages in a child's intellectual development, and that these stages could be related to children's ages. He suggested that as the child developed and matured, one stage would fade, to be replaced by the next one. Piaget's stages are as follows:

Sensori-motor (birth to two): Piaget proposed that children at this first stage are able to deal with this information via their motor skills. They are not yet able to talk, so action is their response to sensory information. A very young baby shows reflex responses to stimuli. The 'startle' response can be seen when a baby hears a very sudden or loud noise. Gradually these responses become more purposeful.

Pre-operational (two to seven years): This stage is characterised by the emergence of symbolic representation: that is, that an object, or picture, can represent something else. Perhaps you have seen children of this age playing with a cardboard box, which is used to represent a boat, car or train. Children at this stage are often described as being egocentric: they are not yet able to see the world from another's point of view.

Concrete operations (seven to eleven years): At this stage, children have to use concrete objects to aid their thinking. They cannot yet think in an abstract way by formulating and testing hypotheses, without any concrete experience on which to base their thinking. At this stage, egocentricity disappears and children are able to see something from another point of view.

Formal operational (twelve years onwards): At this stage, reliance on concrete examples diminishes. Children are able to use logical and hypothetical thinking and can make links between information and concepts to aid their thinking.

Piaget's theories have been used in teacher education for a long time. They offer a systematic framework, in which we can think about when and what to teach children. They are, however, not supported by a lot of recent research. Children as young as five can perform formal operational tasks. Children in nurseries can be taught to consider other children's perspectives. The work of Reuven Feurstein takes Piaget's ideas further.

Practical application: observing children and classrooms

The influence of Piaget can be seen in today's classrooms.

Try to find a time to observe a child or group of children of different ages. Think about the different activities and organisation, and how they reflect Piaget's stages. Some examples are given in the table below to start you off. Opportunities to observe will depend on your circumstances. For example, not many schools will have children under two on the premises, unless there is a crèche or playgroup.

Stage	Example
Sensori motor	1. Putting toys in mouth 2.
Pre-operational	1. Role play areas in Foundation Stage settings 2.
Concrete operations	1. Using counters or cubes in maths work 2.
Formal operations	1. Taking part in a discussion about a moral issue 2.

As well as Fuerstein, two other influential psychologists have contributed to this area, Lev Vygotsky and Jerome Bruner. The work of all three is considered in Part 3 of this book.

Practical application

Cognitive psychology is concerned with how we think. It focuses more on the processes than the products of learning. In the class-room, this means that *learning to be a learner* is important.

When you are working in a classroom alongside a teacher, try to notice how much of the teaching focuses on *learning to learn* skills. Use the table below to help you. An example has been completed for you.

What to do	How to do it
Complete the sums on this sheet.	Look carefully before you start.

Psychoanalytic psychology

No psychology text could be complete without reference to the work of Sigmund Freud and his followers. The term *psychoanalysis* refers to a process which is still used over a hundred years after its creation.

There are a number of fundamental assumptions made by this school:

- There are some processes in our minds which we are aware of and processes that we are not aware of. They are called *conscious* processes and *unconscious* processes

- Our behaviour and thoughts are mainly driven by primitive drives and motives. These are found in the unconscious part of our minds (or psyche) and result in goal driven behaviour. We are not always aware of the goals of our thoughts and behaviour

- Many of our conscious thoughts and perceptions are distorted to avoid anxiety. These are *defence mechanisms* which are designed to protect us from fear

- These defence mechanisms include mental processes known as *transference, projection, displacement, sublimation, denial, splitting, introjection and rationalisation*, amongst others

- Our early experiences are very important in determining how we perceive the world. Early relationships with care-givers are emotionally charged and influence our view of the world

- Asking people to account for their actions will not provide the fullest picture because people are not necessarily aware of what influences their thoughts and actions.

These ideas may seem unusual. This school has generated some of the most contentious debate of all. This example illustrates some aspects of psychoanalytic psychology.

Imagine a four year old child who is placed in a room with a number of sweet things. They are told that they must wait until teatime before they can have the food. The adult leaves the child alone in the room. The child, tempted by the chocolate biscuit, eats one and hides the wrapper by putting it in the empty waste paper bin. Unfortunately, there is chocolate round the child's mouth. The adult returns and sees the chocolate on the child's face and the wrapper in the bin, which was empty when they left the room. 'Have you been at the chocolate?' asks the adult. The child lies and denies it. The adult returns with a 'I think you have...'. From the child's point of view, they can have no idea how the adult knows they are lying, but the adult is well aware of the lie and the motivation behind it.

We have no difficulty understanding how both the adult and child arrive at the position that they are in. In the same way, psychodynamic psychologists can understand how they and their clients arrive at the positions they are in and are happy to generate ideas, or hypotheses, about what might be happening in the unconscious worlds of the clients.

Freud saw the mental lives of children as resolving conflicts between the basic drives, including sexual, and expectations of the society in which the children were raised. The part of the mind (*psyche*) which contained these drives he called the *id*. Actually, he called it the *it* in his native German. Only in translation into English did it take the Greek form. The part of the self which was conscious was called the *ego* and the part which corresponded to the influence of society was called the *super ego*. Freud saw the ego as responding to the conflicts between the id and the super ego.

Critics of the psychodynamic school point out that there is an untested assumption that these unconscious processes even exist, let alone in the form suggested by the psychodynamic school. Sigmund Freud's clients were not children but mainly middle-class women. However, a number of psychologists have extended Freud's ideas. The more modern practitioners emphasise the mental processes rather than the unconscious drives. Melanie Klein worked with children and introduced the concept of splitting into this school of psychology. Children resolve mental conflicts by splitting ideas (or objects) into good and bad. Children will develop different views of the same person. The mother who feeds and cuddles the baby is seen as different from the mother who chastises the child. In the mind of the child there is the good mother and the bad mother. Only with maturity does the child come to the view that they represent different aspects of the same person. The psychodynamic school provides a convincing account of the process of transference. This process can occur between people. We can act in apparently irrational ways with people. This may occur because the person is similar in some unconscious way to somebody else who was important in early life. Practitioners talk about the 'emotional baggage' that we carry around with us.

The ideas in the psychodynamic school provide a way of thinking about the reasons people behave in the ways that they do, but it also provides a basis for therapy. Many people are prepared to pay a great deal, over a great length of time, to gain the kinds of insights offered by this school.

The assumption made by proponents of this school that these unconscious processes are real and therefore scientific is challenged by others who point out that it has not been proved. Furthermore, the method of helping people known as *psychodynamic psychotherapy* is no more successful than many other quicker methods. When studies have attempted to analyse the incidence of adult mental illness by looking at some of the predictions made by this school, they have generally failed to find any. However, the influence of psychology from this school is considerable. Many different approaches to counselling have a psycho-dynamic history. Concepts are found in the general lives of people who might talk of 'getting rid of the anger', 'being in denial' or 'working things through'. What is important is knowing when concepts from this school are being used. In the summer of 2003 there was a discussion about the motives behind the war with Iraq. Some believed that it was a justified response to a dangerous situation, others that it reflected an unconscious need by the USA to express the anger created by the atrocities of September 11th 2001. When people use these ideas, it is important to know that they originated in the psychoanalytic school of psychology.

Some of the fundamental assumptions found in this school are found in others. The importance of early experience is found in *social constructionism*; the understanding that there are behaviours which relate to reproduction are found in the *biological* school. The appeal of the psychoanalytic school is great. It offers a theory of the way the mind works, a way of helping people in distress and a vast array of case studies which make very interesting reading. It has survived and developed for over a hundred years. Critics point out the that the theory is unproven, the method of helping people is no better than other methods and often so expensive and time-consuming that they are inaccessible to many and many case studies are old and based on a very limited sample of people.

In the UK education system there are some explicit applications of psycho-analytic psychology. A few special schools exist which run on psychodynamic lines. The theory behind nurture groups can be found here. In general, they are found in the education of children who do not relate to other children. This is not the case in other countries. In Italy, for example, there is a much greater em-phasis on psychoanalytic psychology in education. Only time will tell how long it survives in the UK.

Question: Do you know anybody who undertook a course of analysis? If so, what did they gain from it?

Other schools of psychology

There are additional schools of psychology which include:

- Marxist
- Feminist
- Emancipatory
- Post Modern
- Critical

At present none of these are used much in schools. However it may well become the case that in the future more use will be made of them. To illustrate the distinct approaches, two situations are examined through different schools of psychology.

The first example is a nine year old who is not learning to read. A *cognitive* psychologist would examine the child's vision and hearing to establish that the child can see and hear the letters and sounds. The child may be given a battery of tests to establish that her brain was processing information in the same way as those of other children the same age. The progress she has made in reading is compared with the progress she has made in other areas. The reading skills are examined. Various conclusions might be drawn such as:

- the child's vision and/or hearing is defective

- the child's memory is poor

- the child is generally slow at learning

- the child is not generally slow at learning, but is slow specifically with reading, writing and/or spelling

A *behavioural* psychologist's approach might be different. After their hearing and vision are checked the child's existing reading skills may be analysed: whether her experience of learning to read had been rewarding or not and the teaching programme she has been given. This may lead to such conclusions as:

- the child lacks certain key skills, such as knowing letter sounds or how to build up words

- the child has not learned some necessary skills to the degree necessary for successful reading

- the child's experience of learning to read has not been positive

- the child's reading programme has been poorly organised or inappropriate.

There is a key difference in the two approaches. The cognitive psychologist examines what may be happening in the child's brain, whereas the behavioural psychologist examines what experiences the child has had and what influences these may have had.

The second example is of an eight year old boy. Jim was sent to a special school when he was seven. His behaviour in his local primary school was very poor. He swore at the adults, disrupted the class and refused to do his work. His handwriting was particularly poor, although he could read quite well. As a result of his poor behaviour he spent a lot of time working outside the class. The headteacher would often have him working in her room to give the class a rest. His mother was raising the boy and his two younger sisters on her own. They lived in a small council flat without a garden. Although money was tight, Jim always came to school in clean uniform. He enjoyed good health. His attendance at the special school meant that he had to catch a special bus laid on by the education authority. He didn't like this because the bus was also used to transport disabled pupils and those with more profound learning difficulties. The other children in the street called him 'spakker'.

A behaviourally orientated psychologist would begin by looking at the rules, rewards and negative consequences associated with his behaviour. It might be that working in the headteacher's room was more pleasurable than working in the classroom. Jim might be misbehaving in order to have time in the more pleasurable place. If a classroom is associated with being told off, avoiding this situation by behaving in a way that results in being excluded from the class makes sense. The intervention might include a programme of rewarding positive behaviour in class.

A psychologist working in a more experientialist way would begin by listening to Jim's experience of education. Jim might be distressed by his journey on a bus which is used for a wide range of pupils. Being teased by other children in the street may be a source of distress. The history of being told off in a classroom might have created a very negative view of education. He may not see that schooling has anything positive to offer. Interventions might include creating opportunities for his teachers to learn more of how Jim sees education and ways of helping Jim achieve his own ambitions through school. Overall, the aim would be to increase communication between all those concerned.

Notice the differences in the ways these different psychologists approach the same situation.

Now you have go!

Hypothetical case study

Consider the following situation. It is fictional, but constructed from a number of real life elements. Which elements of John would be highlighted by the different schools of psychology described above?

John is nine years old. His mother took drugs and drank heavily during pregnancy. There were problems with his birth and he was taken into care immediately after he and his mother were able to leave hospital. Initially he was placed with foster carers who had a great deal of experience with short-term fostering. Unfortunately, they were unable to keep him after a year and he went to different carers. He was finally adopted at the age of three. Whilst in foster care he went to a playgroup, but he was described as 'difficult' with other children. The play group leader asked the carer to keep him at home until he had settled more. His adopted parents sent him to a nursery, but they too said that he was not relating to the other children and was hurting them, although they didn't think that he meant to hurt them. He was trying to play. His parents were offered a place in a special nursery, which catered for children from a wide range of backgrounds. There were many children there who did not relate well to others.

John was sent to his local primary school. The school was aware that he had not been able to go to a local nursery. He did not know the other children at the school, although they had already had a year together and knew each other. They were very good with him and helped him to join in the local activities both in and out of school. However, his teachers described him as 'very active' and 'always on the go'. They noticed that he did not like reading and preferred to play in the home corner rather than listen to a story. At the age of nine he had the reading skills of the average six year old. He was still finding it difficult to sit still in class and occasionally got into trouble for hitting other pupils. The headteacher suggested that the staff and parents might like to talk to a psychologist. They agreed.

Question: What features of the above could be the starting point for:

- A. A biologically orientated psychologist?
- B. A behaviourally orientated psychologist?
- C. A cognitive psychologist?
- D. A psychodynamically orientated psychologist?

Key elements relevant in John's situation:

1. possible biological difficulties due to drug and alcohol abuse by mother, birth difficulties

2. possibly hyperactive

3. the child's pre-school experience. He did not have the same nursery experience as other children and did not know them on arrival at school

4. John opted out of story time, thus reducing his access to literacy

5. John preferred intimacy of the home corner rather than being in the large group of children

6. Possible cognitive difficulties consistent with poor reading

7. Difficulties in bonding to a parental figure during first years of life

8. Parental anxieties about the child and his future

Can you work out which elements (1-7) might be picked out by the different kinds of psychologists (A – D)

Answers:

Biological school (A) 1 and 2
Behavioural school (B)3 and 4
Cognitive school (C)1 and 6
Psychodynamic school (D) 7,8 and 5.

In practice, applied psychology and psychologists adopt the standpoint most likely to help the situation. It would be wrong to suggest that someone working primarily from one school would not use ideas and concepts from another, if this was likely to help the situation. All psychologists are committed to act in the best interests of their clients.

In this book a number of different perspectives will be used. It will be made quite clear which perspective is being used at each point in the text. You may find it helpful to refer back to the relevant section in this chapter in order to understand the thinking behind each approach to different problems.

Summary

■ this chapter offers an overview of different schools of psychology

■ each school has its own starting points and assumptions about what is important about how people's minds and behaviour work

■ each school may adopt different methods when faced with the same problem and may suggest different approaches.

■ all schools of psychology aim to help people and consider their well being to be of paramount importance.

References and further reading

Atkinson, R, Atkinson, R, Smith, E and Hilgard, E. (1985) *Introduction to Psychology* London Harcourt Brace Jovanovich

Sapsford, R. (1996) *Issues for Social Psychology* London Sage

Stevens, R (1996) *Understanding the self* London Sage

2

An Emancipatory Perspective

This chapter

- ■ introduces the concept of emancipatory psychology
- ■ applies this concept to the work of teaching assistants

The Russian philosopher, Karl Marx, is credited with the idea that differences in power have dramatic implications for individuals. In societies where there are inequalities, those with more power use that power to retain their position. There are vested interests for them in keeping the weak in their place. How this occurs can be subtle. Low pay, combined with pressures to spend money on expensive items to keep a position, discussions and decisions being taken affecting the lives of the weak without their inclusion, technical words used so that the powerful can exclude those not familiar or educated in their use. *Emancipatory* psychology seeks to expose these processes so that a more equal society might emerge.

The relevance of these ideas for teaching assistants is clear. Teaching assistants are amongst the lowest paid in education: there are fewer of them than teachers (128 000 teaching assistants compared with 424 000 teachers) and job security is low, with many on part-time and temporary contracts. The vast majority are women – 98 per cent in 2004 – and have few, if any professional qualifications. As such, teaching assistants are vulnerable to processes which exclude their influence. In the introduction to their book, *Untold Stories*, O'Brien and Garner comment that:

> .... Here was another classic case of a group of 'workers' – a largely female group too – being 'done to' by others who were perceived as

being in positions of greater authority and knowledge and therefore able to exercise power over them. O'Brien and Garner (2001)

This book notes that published material available for teaching and learning support assistants didn't include contributions from the teaching and learning support assistants themselves. The language of guidelines for assistants in schools includes 'how to use' or 'how to deploy'. The suggestion behind that assistants are simply commodities. There is an irony in the assumption that assistants are employed to assist in the inclusion of children. How many assistants themselves are included in the decision-making around their roles in schools? How many assistants are included in continuing professional development in an area of learning?

Two psychologists, Kagan and Burton have identified five social trends relevant at this time, as illustrated opposite.

Whilst the last element may not seem relevant to the specific role of a teaching assistant, the first four are. These create challenges to creating a more just and equal society.

Tangible signs of institutions acting in a non-democratic ways include:

- teaching assistants are not being offered contracts
- teaching assistants are being given contracts with very large numbers of expectations or duties
- teaching assistants are not being included in meetings
- teaching assistants are not meeting as a discrete professional group
- teaching assistants are not being included in case discussions
- it is assumed that teaching assistants do non-contractual tasks which are seen as menial (eg making coffee and washing up)
- teaching assistants not being given lesson plans for the forthcoming week
- teaching assistants' views being the last to be expressed at meetings
- teaching assistants not having professional development opportunities
- one school surveyed gave the teaching staff release time to prepare lessons on one afternoon a week by using the teaching assistants to run an 'art afternoon'. However, the teaching assistants are *not* given any preparation time to prepare this work. Moreover, the classroom management required for such an activity is generally more complex than required for activities which involve less movement around the class.

Social Trend	Challenge	Possibilities for resistance	Local Action	Wider Struggle
Inequality	Widening social and financial differences between people	Concentrate energies on those with least power	Discussions with marginalised groups and those with little power	Struggles for social justice and equity
Apparent liberalism	People become commodities which can be traded	Promotion of participation in civil societies	Local groups becoming aware of the trends	Resistance to globalisation and empathy with minority groups
Repression	Increased harshness towards minorities	Promotion of civil and human rights	Form alliances and create new social groups	Lobby against repressive laws
Deregulation and privatisation	Privatisation of public and community facilities and services. Reduction of local accountability through elected bodies	Education	Developments of alternative systems	Anti-privatisation protests
Environmental destruction	Domination of global capital and threats to sustainability	Decision making	Information, education, individual and collective action	Ecological lobbying, direct actions and development of alternatives

Adapted from Kagan and Burton (2001)

Experiences of teaching assistants vary enormously. One wrote:

> I know of cases where LSAs are seen as mere dogs-bodies and domestic supporters, whose responsibility stops at putting on coats at the end of the day. (Amy Hamilton in O'Brien and Garner, 2001)

Another teaching assistant separates the financial from the social aspects. Writing about the treatment they received from supply teachers one wrote:

> ...The teaching assistants work to hold the group together and to keep standards, because they know the children, yet the supply teacher gets so much more money than us. It is not a money issue really, it is a responsibility issue and we have taken most of the responsibility for settling the class and keeping control within the class. There are some good supply teachers, but some see you, and treat you, in a very negative way. (Spencer Burke, in O'Brien and Garner, 2001)

There are other, positive stories. Teaching assistants talking of being valued, included in decision making and being seen as an active contributor in the education of the children.

Challenging the negative practices is not easy, but some are easier than others. The facilitation of professional meetings for teaching assistants can lead to extensive discussions about their role. These discussions construct a debate and through that the development of ideas and principles about their role. When one teaching assistant discovers that another has a timetable and lesson plans for the next week, the information can be put to good use.

However, care needs to be exercised when talking about developing opportunities for teaching assistants. There is a current trend to introduce foundation degrees for learning support work. One publicised attraction of this is the possible progression to a teaching qualification. What message might this send to teaching and learning support assistants? Whilst there may be some would choose to pursue this career path, by no means all will. The hidden message, that learning support is less valued than teaching, can be perpetuated by such ideas.

Emancipation and history

Marxist philosophy considers the impact of power and how it is maintained. Feminist psychology uses Marxist ideas and applies them to women, on the basis that men have occupied more positions of power in history. The processes by which this can occur are not always obvious. An example of one of the more subtle ways in which powerful groups have maintained their power can be found in the presentation of history. In the USA, the history taught in schools was the story of white people, usually men. The heroes of history tended to be white men. Thus, there was a subtle bias towards celebrating the powerful group. One way of promoting equality was to research the history of black people, including women. If we apply these ideas to teaching assistants we find a similar situation. The heroes of education tend to be ministers and high-status teachers. There is no published history of teaching assistants, nor a widespread public celebration of teaching assistants as heroes. When combined with the relatively low pay, compared with teachers, and history of a predominantly female group, we suggest that this is an area ripe for research.

There are two historical strands which are relevant to this work:

■ the history of teaching and the development of adults instructing children

■ the development of inclusive education and the use of adults to support young people with what is now called *special needs*

Some information about both of these subjects follows.

A brief history of teaching

In the early days of compulsory education teachers were in short supply. Classes were big. Older children were used to teach younger ones. Prefects, *praepostors* and monitors were part of teacher's support for many years. There have been programmes in schools which include parents in the teaching of various subjects. The first contracts for teaching assistants working in local authorities were prepared in 1972, following the 1970 Education Act. At the time of writing (2003) there are over 122,000 assistants working in schools in England. This compares with 424,000 teachers. So although the majority of adults working in schools are professionally qualified teachers, more than one in five are teaching assistants. The current interest in providing qualifications for teaching assistants can be seen in different ways. It can be seen as a positive development.

In England, schools grew up in the fourteenth century near the great cathedrals. These served to teach Latin. This gave access to the law, church, government, diplomacy and administration. The teachers would be drawn from the ranks of the pupils who had probably attended one of the older Oxford or Cambridge colleges. Some of the names of these medieval schools are still familiar to us, such as Eton and Winchester. The fame and success of these led to imitation by many smaller schools.

Records of the experiences of pupils are rare, but some illustrate brutality. Their hours were from dawn to dusk. Classes were large and discipline was provided by a stick of birch. There is a record of classes of two hundred pupils being taught by one master. The bigger the classes, the greater the fee. A description of a Dr Keate of Eton suggests that he beat seventy two boys in one session.

> The floor was covered with victims; the benches and tables with spectators ... jeers and laughter accompanied the execution. (Kingslake, quoted in Martin, 1979)

It was not until the sixteenth century that kindness and fun were thought of as being of value to children's development. The seventeenth century saw the questioning of the classical curriculum, Latin was taught by rote. A pamphlet published in 1659 condemns the classical curriculum as:

> ... a show of knowledge like a parrot who speaks words but he knows not what he saith. (Martin, 1979)

Which is the origin of the term 'parrot fashion'.

But cruelty was still rife in the schools at the time. In school at the beginning of the nineteenth century, there was a belief that children were best left to themselves, with minimal interference from the masters. Bullying was rife. A system of fagging evolved. Fagging was derived from carriers of faggots or bundles of wood for open fires. Younger children fagged for older ones. In effect, they became unpaid servants who could be flogged if they did not do the elder pupil's bidding. There are records of fags being branded, burned with cigars and being tossed in blankets. The concept of child abuse was a long way ahead of these times. In 1808, senior pupils at Harrow protested with banners about the removal of their flogging rights. (Not all schools were so generous. The caning of younger pupils by senior prefects or *praepostors* was still to be found in the 1960s.)

The reforms introduced in the early nineteenth century included rethinking the concept of leaving children to themselves. The system of prefects or *praepostors* was actually reintroduced to reduce brutality between children. Masters gave some authority to older pupils to see fair play and good order. Thus, the concept of an assistant to the teacher was born.

However, education for the working classes was not found in large institutions. Anyone could set themselves up as a teacher and dame schools were common until about 1850. A widow or spinster could put a notice outside her door offering to teach reading and writing. Discipline was by a stick and a corner in which to stand the classroom 'dunce', but it was the industrial revolution that led to a huge rise in schools. Children worked in factories, but were free on Sundays. Clergy, and others, used Sundays to teach children. Thus 'Sunday School' became the first, really popular, mass educational opportunity in England.

Glimpses can be gained from contemporary fiction. Charlotte Bronte created the character of Jane Eyre in 1847. Jane attended a boarding school and described her time thus:

> During these eight years my life was uniform: but not unhappy, be-
> cause it was not inactive. I had the means of an excellent education
> placed within my reach; a fondness to excel in all, together with a great
> delight in pleasing my teachers, especially such as I loved, urged me
> on: I availed myself fully of the advantages offered me. In time I rose
> to be the first girl of the first class; then I was invested with the office
> of teacher; which I discharged with zeal for two years: but at the end of
> that time I altered.

So Jane Eyre rose from pupil, to head girl, to teacher. The history of the pro-
motion of pupils to teachers offers fascinating insights into how teachers were
trained. The origins of the current trend to raise the status of teaching assistants
to teachers can be found in nineteenth century teacher-training.

At the beginning of the nineteenth century teachers were in short supply. A
number of educational societies ran along the lines described by Bronte. Previously, teaching in many of the charitable schools was the domain of trades-
people who had failed at their business. Teaching provided a valuable source of
a second income, but there was a move towards qualified or 'certificated'
teachers. An early initiative in this direction came from the monitorial system.
An adult teacher would instruct older and abler pupils, who would in turn pass
on the lessons to the younger pupils. Schools were established in which senior
pupils learned about teaching, but the instruction provided by the monitor was
short and did not raise their general education. However, in the late 1830s it led
to the growth of the pupil-teacher system.

A Glasgow teacher called David Stowe developed a system in which very large
groups of children taught by specially trained teachers who were older pupils
aged between thirteen and eighteen. This led to the development of colleges to
train teachers in these methods. The teachers were drawn from the schools and
required to teach all day. A significant difference between this and the older
monitorial system was that pupil-teachers were required to improve themselves
and continue their own education. They were examined periodically by inspectors and paid a small fee. In addition, there were scholarships for good pupil-
teachers to attend a two-year training course. In Victorian times they were
known as 'Queen's Scholars'. There was an examination for others interested in
teaching, but many pupil-teachers simply continued to teach without any formal
qualification. The teachers were paid by results, leading to a style of tuition
based on drill and rote.

The 1870 Education Act greatly increased the number of pupils being taught but
made little provision for the huge increase needed in the number of teachers. In
Liverpool a trial took place in which pupil-teachers could attend teacher centres
in the evenings and weekends. This was very successful, with many of the parti-

cipants outperforming the Queen's Scholars in the Queen's scholarship exams. An unfavourable report into the standard of teaching in 1888 caused the system of pupil-teachers to be questioned. Teacher training colleges were established and by 1900 there were sixteen offering 1200 would be teachers a career path. By 1911, the teacher-training course was four years long. Teaching was becoming a profession.

The system of payment by results was abandoned in 1898, following a report of the Education Department:

> The school is a living thing, and should be judged as a living thing, not merely as a factory producing a certain modicum of examinable knowledge. (Education Department 1989, in Martin 1979)

In the early part of the nineteenth century, elementary school teaching was the domain of the upper working classes. Educated middle classes might be found in public schools or elite grammar schools. The 1870 Education Act might have created a huge need for teachers, but a generation later (1900) the breakdown of the teaching force was still:

- trained and certificated 32%
- untrained certificated 25%
- uncertificated ex-pupil-teachers 28%
- article 68 teachers 15% (Evans 1985)

This last group was unqualified, but had to be female, over eighteen, vaccinated and approved by the visiting HMI. In other words, more than two adults in five teaching in schools had no formal qualifications.

The professionalisation of teaching continued, as pay and status grew in the twentieth century. By 1944 the freedom allowed to teachers included the ability to adopt their own teaching methods and choose the curriculum. Teachers were not subject to any dictatorial oversight of their work. Any advice or suggestion from a visiting inspector was simply advisory, the teacher could choose to follow it or not. The graduate teacher population grew from 20 per cent in 1970 to 32 per cent in 1982 to more than 90 per cent in 2003. Although there have been many changes in the nature of teaching, the overarching trends have been towards a more highly qualified profession.

The second strand relevant to a history of teaching assistants is the development of inclusive education.

A brief history of inclusive education

Inclusion is a humanitarian and civilising process which extends services and human rights to all sections of the population.

What follows is a sample of some of the events in inclusive education. The terminology of the time has been maintained to illustrate the ideas of the time.

The earliest record of some aid being produced to assist a person with some kind of physical loss concerned Queen Vishpla, who lost her leg in battle and was fitted with an iron prosthesis. She returned to battle. This information was written in Sanskrit between 3500 and 1800 BC and is found in the *Rig-Veda*, an ancient sacred poem of India.

Not all developments were inclusive. In 355 BC, the Greek philosopher, Aristotle said that those 'born deaf become senseless and incapable of reason'. It probably remained a widespread belief until the late 16th century when Girolamo Cardano, a physician who lived between 1501 and 1576 demonstrated that it was untrue.

Some key dates:

1755   First school for the deaf in the world opens in Germany

1760   Thomas Braidwood opens first school for deaf in England

1791   First school for the blind

1847   Provision for mentally handicapped

1865   Provision for physically disabled

1870   Compulsory schooling for all. Special classes are established for children with sensory and physical handicaps

1880   Education Act make attendance at school compulsory until ten

1886   Royal Commission on the Blind and Deaf recommend compulsory education for these groups

1893   Education act endorses above

1896   Committee on Defective and Epileptic children recommends access to education

1899   Education Act empowers school boards to make provision

1902   Education Act abolishes school boards and hands powers over to local borough or county councils

1905   Alfred Binet and Theodore Simon develop tests to determine mental age of children. This is used to help plan educational programmes for children with some kind of educational difficulty

1907   Maria Montessori opens her first school. She developed programmes for children described as *defective* or *ineducable*

1912   Lewis Stern develops concept of Intelligence Quotient (IQ)

1914   Obligatory education introduced for *defective* children

1915   Louis Terman publishes the Stanford Binet intelligence test in the US

1918   Education Act raises compulsory education to fourteen

1921   Testing of children to allocate to appropriate education. Five categories of handicap defined

1936   Maria Montessori publishes *The Secret of Childhood*

1937   Jean Piaget publishes *La naissance de l'intelligence chez l'enfant* (The origins of childhood intelligence)

1938   First Child Guidance Clinic established in Glasgow

1939   B.F. Skinner publishes *The Behaviour of Organisms: An Experimental Analysis*

1944   Secondary education established for all. Eleven categories used to define children (including *ineducable*).

1970   Education (Handicapped Children) Act. Every child has the right to education

1971   Open University has first students

1978   Warnock Report – strive towards integration. The concept of categories of children replaced by *special educational need*

1981   Education Act. Statements of *Need.* SEN and programmes defined. Parental involvement included

1988   Education Reform Act introduces:
National Curriculum
SATs
Open enrolment
Local Management of Schools
Reduced roles for LEAs
(This had the potential to reduce inclusion. Children with Special Needs might have to follow the same educational programmes as all others)

1993   Education Act Code of Practice for SEN

1996   Education Act Tribunals. Gives powers to parents to challenge decisions of LEAs about children's needs

1997   Education Act Exclusion Tribunals. Gives powers to parents to challenge decisions of schools to exclude children

1998   Green and White Papers: *Excellence for All.* Inclusion of all

2002   Disability Discrimination Act applies to schools.
        It becomes an offence to discriminate against children with special educational needs in all schools

The 1970 Education Act brought all children into the educational domain. Education Authorities inherited staff who had previously worked in hospitals or care centres. Few had teaching qualifications as many came from nursing backgrounds. The new Educationally Sub Normal (Severe) ESN(S) schools had to find staff with teaching qualifications and continue to offer employment to existing staff. The concept of a teaching assistant was born again: organisations quickly realised the value of using staff of this kind to work in a variety of schools as this was much cheaper than employing qualified teachers. By 1976 assistants were used in a few mainstream schools to support children with special needs. The Warnock report in 1978, with the subsequent legislation in the 1981 Education Act, emphasised the benefits of integrating children with special needs into mainstream schools. The adoption of educational statements of special need in 1983 gave Local Education Authorities the duties and powers to allocate additional funding for such children. This was often allocated to teaching assistants. In 2004, foundation degrees for teaching assistants were introduced, providing a path to qualified teacher status. In many ways, this represents a return to routes into teaching which increasing professionalisation had closed.

There are similar stories to be told in other areas of education. The huge increase in young people in universities and colleges has created educational opportunities which include more and more people. In 1900 only 0.3 per cent of young people were in education beyond fifteen, in 1996 the figure was 57 per cent of sixteen to eighteen year olds.

Part of the increase in inclusion has been through the use of assistants for teachers. Time will tell how this will help the development of the education system as a whole.

References and further reading

Evans, M. (1985) *The Development and Structure of the English School System* London Hodder and Stoughton

Hyndeman, M. (1978) *Schools and schooling in England and Wales* London. Harper Row

Kagan, C and Burton, M. (2001) Critical community Praxis for the 21st Century. Paper presented to British Psychological Society Conference, Glasgow, March 2001

Martin, C. (1979) *A Short History of English Schools 1750-1965* Hove. Wayland

O'Brien, T. and Garner, P. (2001) *Untold Stories* Stoke on Trent, Trentham Books

Part 2
The Psychology of Human Development

3

Child Development

This chapter

■ provides an overview of the main developmental milestones of physical and sensory development from birth to adolescence

■ gives information about a range of developmental difficulties which teaching assistants may experience in their work

The development of children is shaped by a number of different elements. Traditionally *nature* and *nurture* have been seen as separate influences on child development. However, ideas have now been taken a lot further.

From the moment of conception, the genetic material of a human is established. Our genes determine many aspects of our development including eye colour, hair colour and gender. Other physical aspects of our development, such as height and weight, are influenced by our genes, but other factors are important too. Whilst the maximum height we might achieve is predominantly genetically programmed, it depends on an adequate diet. Other factors influence our development, even before we are born. Smoking during pregnancy has been demonstrated to reduce the supply of oxygen to the growing foetus, thus affecting development. Women who smoke are twice as likely to have a stillborn child. Smoking reduces the birth weight of children and can lead to deficiencies in vital organs such as the kidneys. There is an association with Sudden Infant Death Syndrome (SIDS, known as cot deaths).

The reasons for these deficiencies are simple. The cigarette generates carbon monoxide, which reduces the blood's capacity to carry oxygen. Smoking suppresses the appetite, so pregnant women eat less than they would normally. The influence of the environment is present, even before the baby is born. Even the genetic material is subject to external influences. Mothers who conceive over the age of 35 are more likely to have children with Down's Syndrome than those who are younger. Down's syndrome is genetically linked.

External factors can increase the development of children before they are born. The so called 'hothouse' babies have caused debate in this field. Mothers who play music to their unborn children report that the children appear to recognise and respond to the same music after birth. The claims that this creates musical geniuses have been hotly contested. Critics point out that the children exposed to these sounds tend to come from musical families, who introduce their children to music from an early age. By raising children in a musical environment, they are more likely to acquire musical skills. One of the more unusual centres of musical talent was an orphanage in Venice in the seventeenth century in which Vivaldi, the composer of the *Four Seasons,* worked. The orphanage girls became competent musicians, yet their backgrounds were certainly not musical.

Birth marks the first transition for the baby. Our species has the largest brain to body ratio in the world. The success of mammals on earth owes much to the successful way in which we promote our genes. Protecting our genes by keeping the baby inside the mother, during the early and most vulnerable stages of development, is sensible. Only when the baby's head is so large that further growth would lead to difficulties for the birth does our biology allow the baby into the wider world. It is still highly dependent on its parents to continue its development.

Teaching assistants work with children and young people at all stages of their education, from the Foundation Stage to Key Stage Four. Some also work in a daycare or nursery setting, with children aged three and under.

Whatever the age of the children or young people with whom you are working, it is helpful to have some knowledge and understanding about human development. This knowledge and understanding will help you to know broadly speaking what to expect at different ages and stages and will help you to decide whether to be concerned about any problems, difficulties or challenges that children might present. We can really only determine what is 'abnormal' if we have some idea of what constitutes 'normal'.

Having introduced the notions of normal and abnormal, we should not be rigid in our use of mapping development to ages and stages. Within each age and stage, there is some degree of variability that is normal. Parents well know all those baby books that tell you what your baby should be doing at particular age and then worry because their baby does not match up. Trips to the baby clinic, where you see what other people's babies are doing and then compare them to your baby, are equally revealing. Any developmental information should be used cautiously, particularly if you are working with children under five, since development during the first five years of life is subject to rapid change.

Historical overview

The historical origins of the study of child development outlined in this section continue to influence psychology today. One of the debates that is ongoing in psychology is the nature-nurture debate, in other words, how much of what makes us what we are is determined by our genetic inheritance *nature*, or is shaped by our environment *nurture*? This debate arose from two very different philosophical viewpoints about children and their development.

John Locke (1632-1704) proposed that the young child was a *tabula rasa*; that is, a blank slate. According to Locke, therefore, children develop into unique beings as a result of their experiences. Consequently, Locke suggested that parents should provide an environment that helped this development by, for example, encouraging curiosity and responding to children's questions. The type of education system based on Locke's philosophy was therefore one that placed a responsibility on society to educate and to shape the child in order to become an acceptable member of society. Reward and punishment were emphasised as the means of educating and shaping.

In contrast, Jean-Jacques Rousseau (1712-1778) thought that biology was the most important factor in development. According to Rousseau, the individual that the child develops into is predetermined, consequently adult intervention is not necessary or desirable. The education system based on Rousseau's philosophy, therefore emphasised children as being active in contrast to Locke, where the child was viewed as a passive recipient and where guidance or supervision was not required, since the child's development would quite naturally unfold.

These two opposite philosophical viewpoints are the origins of the nature-nurture debate that continues to exercise the minds of psychologists and is highly relevant to the psychology of learning. Sometimes the relative contribution of nature or nurture is easy to see. For example, humans appear to be 'programmed' to walk and the development of walking will emerge, regardless of the environment although it could be argued that the speed and precision with which the skill develops is helped or hindered by the environment. The issue of language acquisition is less clear cut in terms of nature-nurture. Are we programmed to talk? This debate continues in more detail in the section about language development.

Stages of human development

The extent and rapidity of change in human development varies at different ages. This will be reflected in the way in which Part 2 separates childhood and adolescence in order to map the development that take place. There are broad characteristics of each stage of development which are summarised in the table below. The most rapid changes are seen between birth and five years. Therefore, the first five years of life will be examined in much smaller age-related divisions. The Sure Start publication, *Birth to Three Matters* describes four stages of development between birth and three years. After that, ages are divided in line with the UK education system; that is, the Foundation Stage for children aged three to five, followed by the four Key Stages that cover the period of compulsory schooling from ages five to sixteen.

STAGE	AGES	BROAD CHARACTERISTICS
Birth to three	0-8 months	Heads up, lookers and communicators*
	8-18 months	Sitters, standers and explorers*
	18-24 months	Movers, shakers and players*
	25-36 months	Walkers, talkers and pretenders*
Foundation Stage	3-5 years	Early childhood: Growing independence and assertiveness, curiosity and eagerness to learn, continued rapid physical development as both gross and fine motor develops more skillfully.
Key Stage One	5-7 years	Middle childhood: Growing awareness of others, beginnings of cooperation, more skilful communicator.
Key Stage Two	7-11 years	Late childhood: Being part of a group or team, importance of rules, able to access formal instruction in school.
Key Stage Three	11-14 years	Early adolescence: Who am I? Rapid physical changes as the body matures to adulthood.
Key Stage Four	14-16 years	Late adolescence: Identity established, self certainty, physical maturation largely complete.

*denotes descriptors from *Birth to Three Matters*

The structure of Part 2

Part 2 is organised into two main sections. The first deals with child development in relation to a number of areas: physical development, language development including aspects of non-verbal communication, social and emotional development and intellectual development. The second main section deals with issues and themes associated with child development: theories of attachment and the effects of child abuse.

Physical development

The way in which a child changes physically is the most obvious sign of child development. This section will look at the major physical changes that occur, in three principal stages of human life: pre-natal development, development from birth to five and adolescence. We will then look at some of the difficulties that children might experience with their physical development, together with implications for teaching assistants.

In this section, physical skills are referred to as either fine motor skills or gross motor skills. This is a common way of looking at physical development. Gross motor development refers to large movements such as walking, running or jumping and generally, therefore, involving the legs and feet. Fine motor development refers to small movements such as drawing or threading, generally, therefore, involving the arms and hands.

Prenatal development

Parents will know that entire volumes are devoted to life before birth, for the purposes of this section, we will give just a brief overview of developments that occur from conception to birth. It is important to have some information about this stage of development, since the physical difficulties that children experience are often attributed to problems with pre-natal development.

Pre-natal development is divided into three trimesters, or three month periods. The table below shows the main developments that take place during each trimester.

Trimester	Main developments
First (0 to 3 months)	Rapid cell division, into three main types of cell, which are:
	Ectoderm (sense organs and nervous system develop from these cells)
	Mesoderm (skeleton, muscles and circulatory system develops from these cells)
	Endoderm (digestive system develops from these cells)
	During the first trimester, these three cell types begin to form the systems associated with them.
	Placenta forms. Primitive heart forms.
	Embryo begins to develop a human appearance. Limb buds begin to develop in to arms and legs.
	Sex organs begin to form
	At the end of the first trimester, the embryo has developed into a foetus. It shows spontaneous movement of arms, legs and fingers.

Trimester	Main developments
Second trimester (4 to 6 months)	Accelerated growth, so that head becomes more in proportion to rest of body. Skin forms. Active reflexes. Movement of foetus can be felt by mother. Eyes open at end of the sixth month. Taste buds and sweat glands develop
Third trimester (7 to 9 months)	Cerebral hemispheres of brain very apparent. Final stages of development and growth of all systems. Lots of activity interspersed with quiet periods. Overall increase in size and weight. The foetus is capable of living independently if born at any time during the third trimester.

Birth to five

The child experiences the most rapid changes in physical development during the first five years of life. The newborn baby is physically quite helpless but by the age of five can move around independently and demonstrate skilled motor movements, such as riding a bike, catching a ball or holding a pencil.

The table opposite gives some of the main milestones in physical development from birth to five.

Middle and late childhood

During the first five years of life, the main gross and fine motor skills emerge. Middle and late childhood is the period when these skills are gradually fine tuned. In other words, the child becomes a more skilful mover and user of tools. Gradual increases in height and weight take place over this period, so children's body shape will change. As height and weight increase, so does strength. The other physical change is that milk teeth are gradually replaced by permanent adult teeth.

Examples of the increase in skilful gross motor movements during these two periods of childhood are skills such as riding a two-wheeled bike, hopping and skipping. From the age of seven upwards, many children have sufficient motor control to begin to learn to play a musical instrument, although younger children might also do this. Bat and ball handling skills improve and are more precise and co-ordinated; for example, the child is able to catch a tennis ball, rather than a larger football. Dressing skills, such as doing up buttons and tying shoelaces tend to emerge, as fine motor skills develop. Handwriting and general pencil skills are executed with increasing precision and accuracy.

Puberty

Puberty is the second phase of rapid change in human development, usually from the age of about twelve years onwards. In early childhood, motor skills are

Age	Main physical milestones
Birth to six months	Can turn head
	Can move arms and legs
	Begins to reach and grasp
	Head control evident
	Purposeful grasping
	Can sit with support, sometimes will sit unsupported at this stage
	Can lift upper body when in supine position (on stomach)
	Can roll over
Six months to one year	Sits unsupported
	Can control legs and feet: will attempt to move legs when held in a standing position
	Crawls
	Will pull him/herself up using furniture and will cruise around the room holding on to furniture
	Can transfer objects from one hand to another
	Apposition of forefinger and thumb
One to two years	Walking develops, shows developing ability to walk independently and to be able to avoid obstacles
	Can walk upstairs
	Can kick a ball
	Can run
	Can pick up small objects using a pincer grip, will begin to grasp a crayon and make marks on paper
	Able to build tower of bricks
Two to three years	Can move up and down stairs
	Can ride a tricycle
	More skilful fine motor: drawing recognisible shapes with crayons, threading small beads, manipulating dough to make recognisible objects
Three to four years	Can jump
	Able to balance; for example, can stand on one leg
	Further skilful fine motor development: larger range of recognisible shapes and objects drawn, able to colour and keep mainly within an outline. Begins to form some letters
Four to five years	Can hop and skip
	Can throw, catch and kick a ball
	Can ride a two wheeled bike, usually with stabilisers, is able to pedal
	Can form wide range of letters and can write name. Can copy and draw more complex designs
	Hand preference is usually clear by now

the main change seen from birth to five, as the major skills of walking and eye-hand co-ordination emerge. The physical changes in puberty are mainly related to the transition from childhood to adulthood and therefore involve the maturing of sexual characteristics. At the same time, height and weight increases for both boys and girls, often showing periods of rapid growth.

Hormones associated with male and female sexual characteristics begin to affect the young person. Both sexes will develop body hair (legs, underarms, pubic hair) and boys will gradually develop facial hair. By the age of sixteen, many boys will need to shave facial hair regularly. Both sexes will experience some voice changes, but this is much more noticeable in boys, as their voice deepens. We refer to their voices as breaking, the time when they fluctuate between a deep adult male voice and their childhood squeak. In girls, puberty signifies the onset of menstruation. This can happen prior to the age of twelve (some primary school girls now start their periods), but is typically evident between the ages of twelve and fourteen. In both sexes, hormonal changes are often accompanied by spots, due to the effect of hormones on skin secretions.

Problems with physical development
A wide range of problems with physical development are experienced by children and young people. In the majority of cases, the cause of these problems are pre-natal that is, they occur as the child is developing in the womb. A small number of physical problems occur due to difficulties at birth. You will be likely to encounter children with physical problems, due to the move towards including all pupils in mainstream education. Schools are now required to comply with the 1995 Disability Discrimination Act, part of which stipulates that buildings should be accessible to individuals with mobility difficulties.

This section will give you an overview of the most common types of physical difficulties. We will look briefly at cerebral palsy, spina bifida and dyspraxia.

Cerebral palsy is a condition that occurs as a result of abnormal brain development, usually before birth. The parts of the brain affected are those associated with motor movements. Cerebral palsy is not degenerative and there is no cure; the areas affected will always be affected, although treatment and therapy can help to alleviate some of the symptoms. There are three main types of cerebral palsy. *Spastic cerebral palsy* occurs when the cerebral cortex is damaged. The result is stiff muscles and consequently restricted movement. This is the most common form of cerebral palsy. *Athetoid or dyskinetic cerebral palsy* involves damage to the basal ganglia. This is a large mass of grey matter found in the cerebral hemispheres of the brain and is associated with motor movements. This type of cerebral palsy is associated with jerky, involuntary movements or spasms, as the individual is not able to control muscle movements. Muscles change from floppy to tense. Speech is often affected as the motor spasms affect the tongue and vocal chords. *Ataxic cerebral palsy* is caused by damage to the cerebellum at the base of the brain. Affected individuals have poor balance and spatial awareness. Three terms are used to describe the extent of the effect of cerebral palsy. *Hemiplegia* means that only one side of the body is affected. *Diplegia* means that the legs only are affected. *Quadriplegia* means that arms and legs are affected.

Spina bifida is a neural tube defect that occurs very early in pregnancy. The neural tube forms the brain, spinal cord and spine. Spina bifida means that the neural tube splits when it is developing and that the vertebrae of the spine do not develop. This leaves the spinal cord unprotected and therefore, damage occurs. The damage to the spinal cord affects nerve endings, meaning that the individual affected has no sensation below the level where the damage occurs. The extent of difficulties varies according to the extent of damage. Many individuals with spina bifida are able to walk. Loss of sensation means that there are sometimes continence problems, due to not feeling the urge to pass urine or to defecate.

Dyspraxia is a motor disorder that is related to immaturity in the organisation and planning of movement. *Praxis* means the ability to plan and execute skilled motor movements. Therefore, dyspraxia means an absence of the planning and skill. Dyspraxia differs from cerebral palsy and spina bifida in that there is not a specific neurological disorder arising from damage to or abnormality in a specific area of the brain. In the past, individuals affected might have been called clumsy, or diagnosed as having 'minimal cerebral dysfunction'. Dyspraxia is diagnosed by assessing the child's motor patterns and movements. It can be diagnosed in relation to specific movements; for example, it is possible to have a diagnosis of oral dyspraxia, which involves articulation difficulties and problems in imitating voluntary oral movements such as involving the tongue or lips. Verbal dyspraxia affects the child's ability to co-ordinate the movements needed to produce spoken language and the sequencing of language. Generally speaking, dyspraxia is characterised by delayed motor development and slow and dysfluent movements

Implications for teaching assistants

As stated at the beginning of this section, children vary in their physical development, so it is advisable to be cautious before deciding that there is a problem. Children with specific conditions, such as cerebral palsy, are likely to have received this diagnosis at a very early stage, well before they arrive in a school or nursery setting. As a teaching assistant, you should be working under the direction of a qualified teacher. Therefore, your first point of contact, should you be concerned about a child's physical development, will be the pupil's class teacher, form tutor or subject teacher. You may be employed as a support assistant for a pupil with particular physical difficulties, in which case you are likely to come into contact with health professionals, such as physiotherapists or occupational therapists. Sometimes teaching assistants are employed to implement speech therapy programmes that involve oral movements as a treatment for articulation problems.

If you work with a child or young person who appears to have some co-ordination difficulties, there are some general points regarding support useful as a first step before seeking other advice. These are as follows:

■ allow extra time

■ find alternatives: is it strictly necessary for the pupil to hand write? Minimise the writing load if you can. Use a computer, or act as a 'scribe' for the pupil

■ help the pupil to organise him/herself. This can be a particular issue in secondary schools, where pupils move from one lesson to another and have to take responsibility for noting down homework and having the right materials and equipment for each lesson

■ make sure that tools are appropriate for the job: sometimes motor problems might not be the child's fault! For example, giving a left-handed child a pair of right-handed scissors will not encourage skilled use of this tool

■ provide extra support for routine tasks such as dressing and undressing with appropriate sensitivity to the age of the pupil

Sensory development and difficulties

At the beginning of this section physical development was related to gross and fine motor development. However, it is also important to give a brief overview of sensory development, since problems in this area of development are very common and can have a significant impact on the pupil in school. Sensory development basically covers vision and hearing. We will look at each one in turn.

Vision

Vision involves the development of a range of skills and abilities. As the baby and child develop, the ability to focus increases and the child is able to look at and examine objects in increasingly finer detail. The physical developments we examined earlier in this section also have a visual element. Fine and gross motor development are related to vision. *Hand-eye coordination* describes some of the fine manipulative tasks that children are given. In communication development, a child sees and interpret facial expressions in addition to hearing the words that are said. When children begin to read, they need to have developed quite fine

Types of visual impairment

Myopia
Shortsightedness, caused by the eyeball being too long. This causes problems with distance vision.

Hyperopia
Longsightedness, caused by the eyeball being too short. This causes problems with near vision.

Astigmatism
This is where the cornea (the part of the eye that light passes through) is curved unevenly. This causes blurred vision (but not specifically related to near or distance).

Nystagmus
Involuntary movements of the eye (sometimes known as 'dancing eyes'). It affects the clarity of vision due to difficulties in focusing. The affected individual might tilt their head in order to minimise the visual disturbance.

Optic atrophy
The optic nerve does not transmit properly. The optic nerve sends visual information to the brain. Problems associated with optic atrophy can vary in severity; some individuals have a mild visual loss whilst others might be blind.

Cataracts
A cataract makes the lens of the eye cloudy. Therefore, it is difficult for light to pass through the lens. The visual problems experienced depend on the location of the cloudiness, but in all cases clarity of vision is affected. Photophobia (aversion to light) might also be present.

Glaucoma
A condition where pressure inside the eyeball is raised, due to a failure in the mechanism that drains the fluid away. Glaucoma affects the field of vision and finds it difficult to see when illumination is poor.

Squint
This is where there are problems with the muscles of the eye. If they are not co-ordinated properly, the eyeball is either turned inwards (a convergent squint) or outwards (a divergent squint).

visual discrimination skills so that, for example, they can distinguish between a *b* and a *d*. They also need to have developed visual memory, in order to remember what a word or letter looks like. Colour vision and the field of vision are also important aspects of visual development. Normal vision is described as six/six. The first figure represents the distance that the individual stands from the eye chart in this case, six metres. The second figure is the distance at which the normal eye can see the letters. Six/six therefore means that when the individual stands six metres away from the eye chart s/he can see the letters that it is calculated can be read at this distance (i.e. the six metre letters). The higher the second figure, the worse the vision. For example, vision expressed as six/twentyfour means that letters normally read at a distance of twentyfour metres can only be read at a distance of six metres.

There is an enormous range of visual difficulties. Many children and young people will wear glasses in order to correct a specific sight problem, and provided they wear their glasses will not need to have any additional help or support in and around school. In these cases, the glasses correct the sight so that six/six vision is achieved. However, for some children, their visual impairment is quite significant and even with glasses six/six vision will not be achieved. The box on page 51 contains definitions of the most common types of visual impairment.

Hearing

The ability to hear opens the door to communication with others. If we have difficulties in hearing, we can potentially lose our channels of communication with the world. Therefore, hearing impairment can have a significant impact on the child in school. Alongside the development of the sense of hearing, children develop crucial listening and attention skills. As the child develops, the ability to discriminate and interpret sounds develops. The young baby learns to recognise the voice of their primary carers. The ability to hear is related to scales that measure the loudness and pitch of sounds. Loudness is measured in decibels. A normal conversational voice is usually around 60 decibels and a plane taking off is around 130 decibels. Pitch of sounds is measured in Hertz. Pitch is related to vibration. The more frequently an object vibrates, the higher the pitch. Humans can hear sounds from 20 to 20,000 Hertz. The note *A* above middle *C* on a piano is 440 Hertz. The note *A* an octave higher is 880 Hertz. Therefore, when pitch increases by an octave, the frequency doubles. These values are important in our understanding of a hearing impairment or loss. If an individual's threshold of hearing is reduced by, for example, twenty decibels, they will experience some hearing difficulties. Similarly, if the threshold of Hertz is reduced at either end of the scale, the individual will experience some hearing problems. If the threshold is reduced at the top end of the Hertz scale, the hearing difficulty will relate to high frequency sounds. The reverse is also true; a reduction at the bottom end means that it is difficult to hear low frequency sounds.

There are two main types of hearing loss. A *conductive loss* is one where the transmission of sound from the outer to the inner ear is affected. Therefore, wax in the ear will impair transmission from inner to outer ear. *Glue ear* is a common conductive hearing loss. The normal ear fluid becomes thick, due to an obstruction in the eustachian tube which connects the middle ear to the throat and is usually closed. It opens when we do things like yawn or chew. Enlarged tonsils or adenoids can be a cause of a eustachian tube blockage. Children who suffer from glue ear often have grommets fitted. A grommet is a small valve that is placed in the eardrum. It allows air into the middle ear cavity.

A *sensori-neural hearing loss* occurs when the inner ear or auditory nerve are damaged. This type of hearing loss is thought to be irreversible. However, many children with sensori-neural hearing losses now receive a cochlear implant. The cochlea is the part of the ear that converts the physical energy of sound into electrical energy. It sorts the sounds into different frequencies, then sends messages to the brain. A cochlear implant can be carried out if the cochlea is damaged, but the auditory nerve has to be intact. It involves feeding a wire into the cochlea. The wire has electrodes attached to it, which are tuned to a band of frequencies.

Working with sensory difficulties

It should be clear, even from the brief overviews given above, that the range of vision and hearing difficulties is enormous. If a pupil has a specific vision or hearing problem, specialist advice should be available to schools. Most local education authorities (LEAs) have teams of advisory teachers for sensory impairment. These are teachers who have a further specialist qualification, as either a teacher of the deaf or a teacher of the visually impaired. Many pupils who have significant sensory difficulties are educated in mainstream schools, so teaching assistants are likely to work with sensory impaired pupils at some time. If you suspect a pupil has a sensory difficulty, you can usually ask the school nurse to arrange a hearing or vision test. Screening of hearing and vision is still carried out routinely in schools. The advice for dealing with a vision or hearing difficulty will obviously depend on the type and severity of the difficulty. For pupils who have some sensory impairment not severe enough to warrant any specialist teacher input, a number of common sense steps can be taken. First is to be aware of seating and position in class. Pupils need to sit where there is minimal interference in their vision or hearing, usually at the front of the class and near to the teacher, if hearing is an issue. Pupils might need more time to complete a task with a high sensory input, for example copying from the board. Language might be affected by hearing difficulties, so intervention and support with language would help. Advisory teaching services often produce basic guidelines for dealing with mild vision and hearing problems. The school's Special Educational Needs Co-ordinator (SENCo) will provide this information.

Summary

This section of Part 2 has given an overview of physical and sensory develop-ment, pointing out some of the difficulties that occur when development does not follow normal patterns. The range of difficulties among children and young people varies enormously, from a very mild impairment requiring little addi-tional support, to a severe impairment where the individual might require full-time support in school, in order to cope with the physical demands of the school environment. Not many years ago, children and young people with physical difficulties were usually educated in segregated provision. This is certainly not the case today. More and more physically and sensory disabled pupils are being educated in mainstream schools. Schools are now required by law to make access arrangements to their building for wheelchair users. This means that school staff meet pupils with a range of physical and sensory disabilities and come into contact with a range of professionals, especially health related professions. If you are working with a pupil who has significant physical or sensory difficulties, you will not be expected to cope unsupported. You should have access to specialist health and teaching professionals with a major responsibility for meeting the pupil's physical or sensory needs.

References and further reading

Bee, H and Boyd, D (2003) *The Developing Child (10th Edition)*. Essex: Pearson Academic

Locke, J (1693) *Some Thoughts Concerning Education*

Rousseau, J-J (1762) *Emile*

Sure Start (2003) *Birth to Three Matters*. London: HMSO

The National Association for Special Educational Needs *Spotlight on SEN* series of books are very useful, especially:

Heather Mason *Visual Impairment*
Linda Watson *Hearing Impairment*
Helen Kenward *Physical Disabilities*

These publications are available from NASEN, 4/5 Amber Business Village, Amber Close, Amington, Tamworth, B77 4RP.

4

Language Development

This chapter

- provides overview of the developmental stages of language acquisition

- examines some of the difficulties that children experience with their speech, language and communication

- considers appropriate intervention strategies that can be used by teaching assistants

Language is the main characteristic that separates human beings from other animals. The acquisition of language is one of the most fascinating aspects of a child's development from birth to the early years of schooling. By the age of five, most normally developing children will have acquired a vocabulary of several thousand words and will be able to use quite complex language structures in conversation.

Many classroom assistants are involved in supporting children with language difficulties. An understanding of the way in which language is acquired, the sequence of development and the difficulties that children experience with language should equip you to provide this support.

The purpose of this chapter is to give an overview of theories about language acquisition and development and to look at some of the difficulties that children might experience with language. Finally, we look at practical issues relating to ways of intervening and supporting children with language difficulties and determining when intervention is indicated.

Language acquisition: nature or nurture?

Nature or nurture, already referred to, is one of the key issues in theories about language acquisition. Is language acquisition due to biological and/or genetic factors (nature)? Or is language acquisition due to the environment in which the child is brought up (nurture)? This debate shapes our thinking about how language is acquired, and influences the way we perceive and deal with difficulties experienced by children. The nature/nurture issues also shapes the thinking of the professionals involved in dealing with children's language difficulties, so it is important to have an overview of these theories involved and to know their position in the nature/nurture debate.

Noam Chomsky is perhaps the most well-known psychologist who emphasised the importance of a biological basis for language acquisition. Chomsky proposed the idea of a *language acquisition device* (LAD). The LAD is innate to all children, irrespective of their cognitive development or social circumstances. Children, Chomsky argues, are born with a *universal grammar*, that is, an innate knowledge of the principles of language, mainly related to grammar. This innate knowledge of grammatical principles means that the child is able to generate hypotheses about language. An example of this might be a child who gives the plural of 'mouse' as 'mouses', or who says 'I goed to the park'. In these cases, the child is applying a grammatical rule or principle. This type of speech can be seen as evidence of applying rules and principles as opposed to imitating language that is heard.

Individuals who have suffered brain damage provide further evidence of a biological basis for language acquisition. Studies of brain function indicate that our *language centre* is located in the left hemisphere of the brain. Individuals who suffer damage to this part of the brain often have difficulties with speech and language. A brain injury can affect speech and language. This is evidence for a biological basis.

The theories of **B.F. Skinner** contrasts with Chomsky's. Skinner was in the nurture camp, believing that language was learned through imitation. In Skinner's view, the early beginnings of language acquisition are seen as the parent or care giver reinforces vocal sounds which are close to speech sounds. Later, the child's imitations of language are reinforced and those of most use are therefore retained. Language, according to Skinner, is a behaviour and as such, is subject to the principles governing other human behaviour.

There are problems with both of these views. If we accept a purely biological basis, that there is an innate ability to acquire language, we cannot account for the enormous amount of vocabulary that is learned. If we think that the basis for language acquisition is imitation and reinforcement, this does not explain how children apply a grammatical principle as suggested by Chomsky.

The theories of **Jerome Bruner** about language acquisition are a combination of the nature/nurture arguments. Bruner proposes that children are predisposed to learn language, but that the ability to do so is related to their social context. For Bruner, language acquisition is related to language use in meaningful social contexts. He proposed the idea of the *Language Acquisition Support System* (LASS). The LASS is the social system within which the child learns language. In the early years, this is usually the family. Within the family system, opportunities for language are provided by family rituals and routines, for example mealtimes and bath time. The psychologist **Lev Vygotsky** also emphasised the social aspects of language acquisition. His notion of the zone of proximal development (ZPD) is discussed on page 133. When this notion is applied to language acquisition, it means that interactions with a more skilled communicator help the child to move to the next level of language development.

Both Vygotsky and Bruner emphasise the relationship between language and thought. One of the key developments which takes place as children enter formal schooling is concerned with the relationship between language and thought. Thought is a type of *inner speech* and its emergence is dependent on the acquisition of language. Through thought, or inner speech, we direct our actions. Language also helps us to move from the concrete to the abstract. Piaget's theories, where the move from concrete to formal operations would coincide with the child's transition from primary to secondary education, is a similar transition.

Moving on from the nature/nurture debate: an interactive model of language acquisition

The theories outlined above make a contribution to our understanding of the way in which language is acquired. However, more recent theories about language acquisition have tended not to come down on one side or the other in the nature/ nurture debate. There is now more emphasis on an interactive model of language acquisition, where the importance of everyday social interaction is recognised. These theories are probably closest to Bruner or Vygotsky's notions about language. There is an increasing recognition that pre-linguistic skills play a major part in shaping the acquisition of language. Pre-linguistic skills emphasise pragmatics, that is, aspects of language concerned with the contexts for language, tools for conversation and language as a means of communication. Therefore, there is more emphasis on language as a communication tool than on linguistic aspects of acquisition related to vocabulary or grammar. An example of an interactive emphasis is that of motherese. In this model, language is acquired through interaction. In these interactions, the adult adjusts his or her language use when speaking to the child. The adjustments made are to the tone and pace of speech, to the sentence structure so that more short, simple structures are used, to the amount of repetition and to reference to concrete objects. Therefore, in this

---

An example of 'motherese'

Mark [looking out of the window at the birds in the garden]: Jub Mummy.

Mother [inviting Mark to extend his own meaning]: Oh yes, birds. What are they doing?

Mark: Jubs eat.

Mother [extending Mark's meaning]: Oh, look! They're eating the berries, aren't they?

Mark: Yeh.

Mother [extending and paraphrasing]: That's their food. They have berries for dinner.

Mark: Oh.

(Adapted from Wells, 1986)

---

model, there is a reciprocal relationship between the child as a language learner and the adult as the model.

So what is language and how do we acquire it?

As our knowledge of the function and structure of the human brain increases, it is clear that there is some biological or organic basis for language. Sophisticated equipment for examining brain function shows that language is associated with activity in particular parts of the brain. In addition, we have already seen that a trauma or injury to the brain can mean that speech and language can be lost, even when these were intact prior to the injury. However, the social nature of language cannot be ignored. A *best fit* view of language acquisition would argue that whilst nature gives us the biological predisposition, nurture is the element which triggers the biological factors and turns us into skilled and competent communicators. Therefore, language is acquired through socially meaningful contexts and is based on interaction and communication, via a reciprocal relationship with more skilled language users where the more skilled language user makes adjustments according to the level of the child.

The question of *what is language?* is also important. The theories we have looked at give us some clue, depending on where each theory stands on the nature/nurture/social interaction continuum. For example, Chomsky's LAD emphasises grammar as the underlying aspect of language, whereas Vygotsky's and Bruner's views emphasise language acquisition in an interactive, social context. However, we have considered that both biology and environment play a part in language acquisition. Therefore, to answer the question *what is language?* we need a definition that does not exclude either nature or nurture. Bloom and

Lahey's (1988) view of language is helpful here. They describe language in terms of form, content and use. This way of looking at language takes account of the physical and biological aspects of language acquisition such as knowledge of syntax and the means of producing language and takes account of the social context in which language is learned, such as how the content of language is determined by the language culture and use of language. Therefore, Bloom and Lahey's view is a neutral stance in relation to its biological origins. There are very possibly biological and organic factors which contribute to the development of language form and content. Inclusion of use in our view of language takes account of the social contexts for language acquisition. Each aspect of form, content and use is described briefly below.

Language form involves three aspects of language. These are:

- *phonology*: the pronunciation system of language, concerned with speech sounds involved in producing language

- *morphology*: the structure of words

- *syntax*: The grammatical structure of language

Language content is concerned with the meaning of language, or *semantics*. It involves knowledge of objects, for example, being able to label a cat, dog or horse, relationships between objects, for example, the cat sat *on* the mat) and event relations, for example, the cat sat on the mat *yesterday*. Language content also involves the topics of language, that is, what we talk about. This aspect of language content involves the vocabulary that is used. Categorisation is an important aspect of language content. It is like a mental filing cabinet. It helps us to make sense of the world, by relating new information to what we know already. For example, if we are told or can see that a fnarr has four legs and a tail, we use categorisation skills to put this in the category *animals*. Knowing the characteristics of this category helps us to deal with new examples and information.

Language use is often called *pragmatics*. It involves how we use language to achieve what we need, the social contexts for language and how we respond to language. Pragmatics involves skills such as turn taking, responding to and maintaining a conversation and using a range of language functions to meet our needs.

How do we learn language?

The previous sections covered some of the theories about how humans acquire language and have shown that there is not a clear or convincing argument for either nature or nurture in the acquisition of language and that it is likely that both play a part. We will use Bloom and Lahey's (1988) analysis of language.

They suggest that language is defined as the *integration* of form, content and use: 'For individuals using language and for children learning language, the components of form, content and use come together in understanding and saying messages.'

Having reached a view of what language is, the next step is to think about how it develops. An overview of the way in which language develops will help to understand some of the problems with language development which may arise at school.

The table on pages 62 and 63 gives an outline of the development of form, content and use.

So far in this chapter, we have focused on the acquisition of language, with the developmental sequence ending at five. At this age, the process of *acquiring* language is largely complete; however, the *development* of language skills continues throughout childhood and adolescence. Speaking and Listening is one of the core areas of the National Curriculum. Therefore, throughout all Key Stages, there is an emphasis on promoting the development of these skills. It is beyond the scope of this chapter to go into detail about the way in which the Speaking and Listening National Curriculum Programmes of Study are delivered, since our focus is principally on the process of acquiring and developing language, in order to understand more about the difficulties that children may experience.

Augmented or alternative communication

Language does not always involve the spoken word. For some individuals, it is not possible to use words to communicate. There are a number of alternative means of communication, which you might come across in the course of your work. This section covers some of the principal means of augmented or alternative means of communication.

British Sign Language (BSL) is often used by deaf or hearing impaired individuals. It is a system of manual communication. BSL has its own language structures and is recognised as a language in its own right.

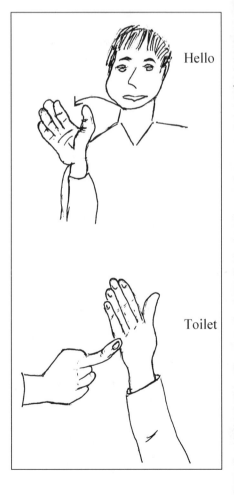

Hello

Toilet

Example of two BSL signs

Makaton is also a system of manual communication. Unlike BSL, the signs used in Makaton are used to represent whole words, and the spoken word always accompanies the sign. It is often used with children who are not developing spoken language, but who do not have any significant hearing impairment. Makaton is used in special school settings which make provision for children with complex and profound learning difficulties.

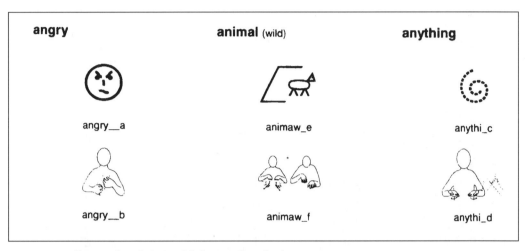

Example of three Makaton Symbols

The Picture Exchange Communication System (PECS) is a communication system which uses pictures or symbols as the means of communication. PECS is based on a behavioural approach, in which the child is taught to exchange a symbol for a desired object The starting point in the initial exchange is usually related to food). There are six structured phases of PECS, with the aim that the child communicates independently. PECS is often used with children diagnosed with an *autistic spectrum disorder* (ASD), on the basis that these children are thought to be visual learners.

Communication aids are sometimes provided for children who are unable to produce speech, for example, as a result of *cerebral palsy*. These aids can be electronic or computer-generated. A screen or control panel is touched in order to activate recorded speech.

Example of six PECS

	Form	Content	Use
0 to 3 months	Crying and vocal sounds Cooing Responds to caregiver's voice and responds to tone of voice (e.g. if being comforted). Begins to distinguish speech and non speech sounds (e.g. turns/moves head when speech heard, shows startle response to other sounds)	Noises are initially unintentional, but early language content relating to personal needs (e.g. hunger) begin to emerge as the carer responds contingently to the sounds made by the baby	Non-verbal gaze fixing Smiling Early non-verbal turn taking
3 to 6 months	Sounds made are closer to speech sounds; e.g. consonant and vowel sounds such as 'ba', 'ga' Laughter like sounds Responds to changes in tone of voice	More intentional sounds and babble, relating to hunger, tiredness, discomfort Begins to respond to name Responds to 'no'	Responds to an interaction, for example, by smiling
6 to 9 months	Babbling, constant repetition of speech sounds, following the intonation patterns of speech Wider range of speech sounds and syllables can be heard in babble Increased recognition of differing intonation.	Growing relationship between sounds produced and particular objects Recognises names of familiar objects and people (e.g. 'mummy' 'daddy'), usually by looking Anticipates familiar events (e.g. being tickled)	Listens when spoken to Turn taking, via games such as 'peek-a-boo'
9 to 12 months	Imitates sounds Babbling continues, with increase in speech like sounds (e.g. mamama) Responds to words and simple commands, rather than just voice intonation.	Content/topics relate to familiar objects and events, such as greeting or departure Will also request (usually non-verbally), such as putting arms up to be picked up	Intentional eye contact Recognises some facial expressions More active participation in turn taking
12 to 18 months	First recognisable words emerge with babbling still present Imprecise or simplified speech production; for example, substitution or omission of initial or final consonants	Object labelling Requesting Meaning conveyed via change in intonation	Begins to give verbal responses to interactions Initiates and terminates interactions

Age			
18 to 24 months	Single words still principal language form, with rapid vocabulary development. Some phrases evident, with changed word order and intonation to convey different meanings, for example, 'mummy go'; 'where mummy?' Pronunciation not always accurate, often with substitutions, but can recognise differences between his/her pronunciation and a correct model	Language content and vocabulary growth related to familiar objects and events. Uses known object labels for similar, less familiar objects. For example, 'parrot' might be used in response to a picture of another bird	Continued development of verbal interactions. Can sustain an interaction for more than one turn
2 to 3 years	Use of tenses. Will understand most types of sentence structures. Uses personal pronouns. Uses plurals. Vocabulary continues to grow (almost 300 words by 30 months)	Interactions not always related to the present: begins to talk about past and future events	Will initiate using vocative (for example, 'mummy!')
3 to 4 years	More consistent use of tenses. Speaks in short sentences with correct syntax. Continues expansion of vocabulary (900 words by age 3, up to 1500 by age 4). Uses possessives and some contractions of words. Uses irregular words (such as use of feet as the plural of foot), rather than over generalising a grammatical rule. Uses conjunctions (but, then)	Asks questions. Uses prepositions. Language content can also include reference. To emotions. Sequence apparent in language topics	Can sustain a simple conversation. Begins to use language in role play
4 to 5 years	Phonology/pronunciation of consonant sounds developed fully. Uses longer sentences with appropriate grammatical structures. More use of words with irregular grammar. Phonological awareness emerging: for example, recognition and use of rhyming words, identification of words with same initial phonemes	Can describe events that take place in different contexts. Can retell a story	Interactions sustained for increasing number of turns. Alters language according to the audience

Linguistic diversity and the impact of schooling

The issue of linguistic diversity is an area which can potentially cause further confusion over the difficulties children experience with language, and whether they should be considered as having special educational needs. Language in nursery or school settings is sometimes very different from the language the child experiences at home. Research carried out by Tizard and Hughes shows that children initiate a great many interactions at home. In contrast, when children are in an educational environment, the types of interactions are very different. Adults tend to dominate interactions, with far fewer opportunities for children to initiate. Instructions and requests are the major language model of practitioners. Questions also feature, but the majority of questions are closed rather than open ended. For many children, the adjustment to this different style of interaction can be very difficult, so that children may be regarded as having language problems, when in fact the problem is more to do with a mismatch between home and school language. It is important, therefore, that practitioners do not make assumptions about a child's linguistic background. The emphasis on partnership in the Foundation Stage Curriculum is a helpful reminder that working with parents in the early years of schooling makes a major contribution to the impact of early education.

Activity: looking at language in different contexts

Although this activity is focused on the Foundation Stage (that is, children between the ages of three and five years who will be in a Nursery or Reception class), it will be useful for assistants working with older children to do this. You will obviously need access to a Nursery or Reception class in the setting where you work.

Practitioners working in early years settings are likely to be working with children who are still acquiring language. An understanding of the way in which language is acquired and developed during the Foundation Stage years is an important starting point.

Choose two half hour slots when you can be free to carry out an observation in your setting.

Choose a child to observe.

Observe the child in a play setting, and note down the language that the child uses.

Then observe the child in a more formal, adult led setting and again note down the language that the child uses.

Are there differences between the language used by the child in each setting? If so, what are they?

Look at the results of your observations in conjunction with pages 19 to 22 of the Foundation Stage Profile. What implications are there for the range of contexts in which a child's language development and progress should be observed and recorded?

It is important to remember that the language children use in school might not show the range of their language competence. There is a danger in making assumptions about a child's language when we only encounter the child's language in particular contexts, or when their language differs in some way from ours. This may involve issues related to accent and dialect.

Many children in school learn English as an additional language (EAL). It is outside the scope of this chapter to cover all the issues involved in emerging bilingualism. If you are working with EAL children, further reading is suggested. In the context of this chapter, where our examination of language acquisition and development is focused towards supporting children with difficulties, it should be emphasised that EAL children should never be automatically considered as having special educational needs. Learning English as an additional language is not a learning difficulty. Where there are concerns that an EAL child might have a learning difficulty, it is crucial to make sure that this difficulty cannot be attributed solely to the fact that English is not the child's first language. A bilingual assessment is a useful first step in trying to determine relative competencies in the child's first and second language.

Difficulties with language acquisition and development

Teaching assistants are likely to meet children who are experiencing some problems with their language development. *Afasic* (a voluntary organisation highlighting the needs of language impaired children) estimates that six in every 100 children will have speech, language or communication difficulties. one in 500 children will experience severe or long term difficulties. This means that if you work in a one form entry primary school with up to 200 pupils, there may be at least one child in each class who has some kind of difficulty.

Children experiencing difficulties with language fall into two main groups: language *delay* and language *disorder*. A language *delay* means that the child's acquisition of language is following the same developmental sequence, but at a slower pace than the majority of children. A language *disorder* means that a specific area of language acquisition is affected, with development not following the expected sequence. Language delays and disorders affect the two major aspects of language: *expressive* language, which is what is said, and *receptive* language, which is what is understood. Language-delayed children often show delayed development in both expressive and receptive language, although their understanding can be more advanced than their expression In the normal sequence of development, understanding develops in advance of expression. A language disorder often affects either expression or reception, with the unaffected area at age-appropriate levels. Language disorders can mean that one aspect of form, content or use is affected.

Children with language disorders are usually given a specific diagnosis. The table opposite is a glossary of some of the labels used for a range of language disorders. They will be used if the child is seen by a medical professional such as a paediatric consultant, or a paramedical professional such as a speech therapist. The table also indicates whether the label describes a disruption of form/content/use and expression or reception.

Although it is useful to know the meaning of the labels used to describe the range of language disorders, these do not necessarily explain how to help the child. If you are confronted with a diagnosis or label, it is vital to ask what it means and what are the implications for helping the child. The use of labels such as those in the table above, is a reflection of the nature/nurture debate. The medical or quasi-medical terminology used places an emphasis on some kind of biological or organic cause for the difficulty. Whilst it is entirely possible that this is the case because individuals who have an injury or trauma to the brain can have impairments of specific aspects of speech or language, it is not always possible to identify a specific cause. Sometimes the diagnosis is inferred from the difficulties presented by the individual. However, there are also often specific strategies which are appropriate for helping a child with a particular disorder. You should seek advice from your school's allocated speech therapist. Most NHS Trusts will have a Speech Therapy Department, which will include paediatric speech therapists, who are speech therapists who work primarily with children.

Intervention in language difficulties

The purpose of this chapter, and indeed this book, is not to provide a series of teaching hints or tips for teaching assistants. Therefore, in the context of looking at difficulties with language development focus is on broad principles which are based on the psychological models we have already considered.

It is important to remember that there might not be any special or different way to promote the acquisition and development of language, particularly when development is delayed. Good teaching practice is effective with SEN children, as long as attention is paid to matters such as pace of instruction, size and type of task and the context in which teaching takes place.

A definition of language was offered for theories about language acquisition:

> language is acquired through socially meaningful contexts and is based on interaction and communication, via a reciprocal relationship with more skilled language users (where the more skilled language user makes adjustments according to the level of the child).

Any consideration of the difficulties experienced by children should reflect this definition. Basically, language is not a skill that develops in a vacuum. There are important contextual aspects to language that should inform the way in which

Label/diagnostic term	Explanation	Main aspect of language affected
Aphasia or dysphasia	An overall term for speech or comprehension difficulties	N/A (generic term)
Agnosia/auditory agnosia	The inability to recognise speech (as distinct from other sounds)	Reception Expression sometimes also affected, as the child does not learn language from models heard. Form, content and use
Cluttering	Rapid speech which interferes with meaning	Expression Language form (phonology)
Dyspraxia/oral dyspraxia	Difficulties associated with the motor movements required for speech production	Expression Language form (phonology)
Dysarthria	Slow and laboured speech. Intonation often poor or inappropriate	Expression Language form (phonology)
Echolalia	The child echoes words or phrases	Reception Language content and use
Mutism	A child who does not speak. An *elective mute* does not speak in any environment or context. A *selective mute* chooses to speak or not to speak in specific environments or contexts (for example, at home but not at school). A *protective mute* does not speak in specific contexts or situations (for example, in the playground)	Expression
Perseveration	Similar to echolalia, but with frequent and inappropriate repetitions	Reception Language content and use
Semantic pragmatic disorder	Difficulties with language use and/or with extracting meaning from language. Affected children often have good language form, but do not use these in meaningful or appropriate contexts	Reception Language content and use
Stuttering	Dysfluency in producing language	Expression Language form (phonology)

we intervene. The implication for intervention is that any language taught should have some utility for the child. Furthermore, language is merely the tool we use to communicate and interact with others. Therefore, when implementing language programmes, issues surrounding use are an important consideration. The usefulness of any language programme depends on whether the child uses the language taught in their everyday communication. The psychology of learning helps us to understand why this is important. A hierarchy of learning can be applied to language acquisition, as shown in the chart below.

The learning hierarchy and language learning

Stage of hierarchy	Implications for language learning
Acquisition Pupil performs a skill accurately	Child imitates a model of desired language Teaching has a narrow focus on 'drills' in order to directly teach the desired language Child produces desired language after prompting This aspect of teaching might take place in a one to one setting
Fluency Pupil performs the skill accurately and fluently	Frequent repetition of teaching of desired language. High level of reinforcement when desired language produced Make sure that there are opportunities for frequent practise
Maintenance The pupil reaches a proficiency level in the skill and maintains accuracy and fluency	Frequent opportunities to use the desired language, perhaps giving teaching opportunities in a small group as well as in individual teaching
Generalisation With instruction, the pupil is able to use the skill in different contexts	The pupil now uses the language in a variety of contexts(for example, in a whole class discussion, during play, during break time), but might need some initial prompting or input about use of the desired language in these settings
Adaptation Without specific instruction, the pupil is able to use the skill in different contexts	Child uses desired language spontaneously in a wide variety of contexts

The implication of this information is that the ultimate goal for language learning is spontaneous use. This is the only way that the language taught has any value or use for the child. This means that assistants should resist the temptation to teach language only in an individual setting, since it is likely that language learned in this setting will not be generalised to the contexts where it is most appropriate.

Incidental teaching is an example of an approach to intervention in language difficulty that addresses the issue of generalising language skills. It was developed in the 1970s by two US researchers called Hart and Risley. In the course of their work, they had contact with children who were experiencing language acquisition difficulties. These children were taught language in a small group which was separate from the rest of the children in the nursery. Hart and Risley found that the small group of children did not use any of the vocabulary they were taught in other contexts in nursery. For example, they were taught colour words in their small group, but did not request objects or materials using colour words. Hart and Risley therefore developed a teaching sequence called Incidental Teaching. This sequence was designed to be used in play settings, where the children had to request materials or objects. The first step in implementing this sequence was to arrange the teaching environment so that children had to ask for objects or materials. Hart and Risley thought that by creating a situation where children had to ask for what they wanted, they were more likely to initiate language that had meaning or purpose for them. Once this had been set up, the Incidental Teaching sequence could be used. The box below illustrates the sequence:

Incidental Teaching

Focus attention	Say the child's name
Model	Give the child a model of the desired language if you think s/he cannot produce it
Ask for elaboration	Ask the child for a more elaborated form of language, or for a particular word that s/he needs to use. For example, if your focus is on colour words, you might say 'what colour do you want?'
Prompt	If the child does not respond to the previous step, give a prompt to help elicit the desired language (for example, 'do you want the red or yellow one?)
Instruct	If the child does not respond to a prompt, give the desired language and ask the child to imitate
Confirm	Give positive feedback ('that's right, well done')

Incidental Teaching is an example of a *behavioural* approach. In the introductory chapter, this approach was summarised it in terms of the ABC analysis of behaviour (A=antecedents, B=behaviour, C=consequences). The initial arrangement of the teaching environment is an example of the manipulation of the antecedents, or setting events. The response that the child receives (the confirm step, always a positive response) is an example of a consequence, which is applied in order to increase the likelihood of the behaviour being repeated.

The box below gives an example of the way in which Incidental Teaching might be used:

Example of Incidental Teaching

Focus of teaching: colour words.

Arrangement of teaching environment: in a sand play activity, different coloured buckets and spades will be used. These will be kept to one side by the adult, so that children have to ask for the sand play equipment.

The teaching sequence will then go like this:

Focus attention	'.................[child's name]'
Model	'we've got red and yellow spades today'
Ask for elaboration	'what colour spade would you like?'

If no response to the ask for elaboration step, then:

Prompt	'do you want a red one or a yellow one?' [hold up two spades]

If no response to the prompt, then:

Instruct	'a red one. You say red spade' [child imitates]
Confirm	'that's right, well done' [hand spade to child]

The main messages from this consideration of language difficulties can be summarised as follows:

- ■ a diagnosis or label is only helpful if it tells you something about how to intervene

- ■ language learning does not take place in a vacuum. Therefore, it is important that socially meaningful contexts are used to help children to learn language

- ■ language is more likely to be learned if has some meaning and value for the child

■ language taught is unlikely to be used if there are no opportunities for generalisation and adaptation

Non-verbal communication

So far, we have looked in detail at the acquisition and development of language. However, if we think about the individual as a communicator not just as a user of spoken language, we need to take a much broader view. This is where the subject of non-verbal communication arises.

It is a cliché, but the saying 'actions speak louder than words' is certainly true. Just over half of what we communicate is non-verbal, that is, without any words used to convey the message. Our non-verbal behaviour tells our audience what we are *really* thinking and feeling! Non-verbal behaviour is basically the way in which we communicate without using words. There are a number of aspects of non-verbal communication:

Eye contact: The eyes have been described as 'windows to the soul'. They can say a great deal about our thoughts and emotions. The way in which we offer and maintain gaze is a powerful means of communication. For example, think about how you feel if you are speaking to someone and they don't look at you. You probably interpret their behaviour as disinterest. Aversion of gaze when someone is speaking, might indicate that they are not being entirely truthful. High-status individuals tend to give and take away eye contact. They break eye contact by looking upwards rather than downwards. However, we need to be careful when interpreting eye contact. Recent research suggests that children tend to avert their gaze when they are thinking. Lack of eye contact is often listed as one of the indicators of difficulties associated with an autistic spectrum disorder (ASD) and can often lead professionals or parents to jump to conclusions about the nature of a child's difficulties. Avoiding eye contact is not the only indicator of ASD.

Posture: If we stand tall rather than slouch we are likely to be thought of as confident and assertive. When we listen to someone, our posture conveys our level of interest. For example, if we have an 'open' posture (open hands and palms, for example) or if we lean forward, we are conveying interest.

Facial expression: Our faces convey our emotions, feelings and state of mind more powerfully than words. We learn to recognise emotions such as anger, fear and happiness when we look at others. We do not usually have to be taught this recognition, but learn the 'rules' through experience.

Personal space: It is difficult to define one's area of personal space. However, we know almost instantly when it has been invaded. It is important to be aware of this when working with children and young people. Invading their personal space, even if it is well-intentioned, can feel very threatening. Use of space can also relate to the way in which we organise our work area. Think about the sort of message conveyed by a teacher who creates a barricade of books and materials around his or her desk!

Dress and appearance: These are quite tricky areas, as they can be very subjective. However, we do make judgments about others on the basis of these factors. Think about the differences between the clothes you wear for work and what you wear to go out with friends. There are probably differences. As with personal space, we know when aspects of dress and appearance are inappropriate. This area also raises issues about body image and assumptions that can be made on the basis of our bodily appearance. For example, we might assume that an overweight person is lazy or not very clever.

Paralanguage: This means the way in which we speak. The tone and volume of our voice helps to convey our message. Also, the vocal sounds we make when we are taking part in a conversation, we make sounds like 'mmm' that convey our continued interest and encourage the speaker to continue.

The implications of non-verbal communication

As a teaching assistant, your job involves contact with other people on a daily basis. Some of these individuals are colleagues and others are the pupils with whom you work. Non-verbal communication plays a big part in the way you relate to others and how you are perceived by others. For example, if you are feeling anxious about working with a particular pupil or group of pupils, you may give out non-verbal signals that show this, such as a higher pitched voice, a frown, a closed or bent posture. Your pupils might be adept at reading these signs, so be aware of what you might be giving away! However, if you know what high status non-verbal signals are, you can practise giving them. Think about a tall, open posture, a calm and even tone of voice and giving and breaking eye contact.

Sometimes our non-verbal signals can be intimidating or threatening. This is particularly the case with personal space and tone of voice. It is important to be aware of the non-verbal signals we are giving, since these will affect the pupil's attitude and behaviour towards us. We should also be aware of non-verbal behaviour in terms of interpreting the non-verbal signals and behaviour of others.

Application activity: non-verbal behaviour

For this activity, you will need to carry out an observation in a classroom.

Choose a class to observe.

First of all, look at the teacher. What is your opinion of their relationship with the pupils? List the non-verbal signals and behaviours that lead you to have this opinion.

Now look at the pupils. What do you think they think of the teacher and the lesson? List the non-verbal signals and behaviours that lead you to have this opinion.

Summary

In this section, we have

- looked at a number of theories about language acquisition

- arrived at a definition of language that incorporates both nature and nurture, and which looks at language in terms of form, content and use

- been given a developmental sequence for the acquisition of language

- looked at some issues surrounding linguistic diversity

- looked at the difficulties that children experience in acquiring and developing language

- looked at the role of non-verbal communication

Try some of the application activities contained in the box below. These will give a practical focus for considering some of the issues that have been covered in this chapter.

Application activities

Identify a child with language difficulties. You might already be working with one of these children. If not, look at the school SEN record or ask the SENCo. When you have done this, try all or some of the following:

- Look at the child's IEP (individual education plan). What aspects of language are being targeted? Can you match these to form, content or use?

- Does the child have a label or diagnosis? If so, what does this tell you their difficulties?

- What does the IEP say about how teaching will be carried out? Does it contain anything about generalising language? If not, think about how you would do this for the particular child.

- Observe the child in class. Note down any evidence of use of the targeted language and any opportunities given for use of the targeted language.

- Use the Incidental Teaching sequence to plan a language-based session with the child. Carry out your teaching session and note down the outcomes.

- Talk to the speech therapist allocated to your school. What are their views about language acquisition? What does s/he think about ways of promoting language acquisition and development in a school context?

References and further reading

Bloom, L and Lahey, M (1978) *Language Development and Language Disorders.* New York John Wiley

Bruner, J (1983) *Child's Talk: Learning to use Language.* New York Holt, Reinehart and Winston

Chomsky, N (1959) A review of B.F. Skinner's Verbal Behavior. *Language*, 35, 1, 26-58

Chomsky, N (2000) *New Horizons in the Study of Language and Mind.* Cambridge: Cambridge University Press.

Hart, B M. and Risley, T R (1975) Incidental Teaching of language in the pre school. *Journal of Applied Behavior Analysis,* 8, 411-420

QCA (2000) *Curriculum Guidance for the Foundation Stage.* London: HMSO

Skinner, B.F. (1957) *Verbal Behavior.* New York: Appleton

Tizard and Hughes (1984) *Young Children Learning: Talking and Thinking at Home and at School.* London: Fontana

Vygotsky, L S (1978) *Mind in Society.* Cambridge, Massachusetts: Harvard University Press.

Wells, G. (1986) *The Meaning Makers: Children Learning Language.* London: Heinemann

Useful organisations

Afasic 2nd Floor, 50-52 Great Sutton Street, London EC1V ODJ
www.afasic.org.uk

ICAN 4, Dyers Buildings, Holborn, London, EC1N 2QP
www.ican.org.uk and www.talkingpoint.org.uk

5

Social and Emotional Development

This chapter

■ gives an overview of the main developmental milestones for social and emotional development, from birth to adulthood

■ introduces attachment theory

■ discusses the roles of families in the development of children

■ describes the impact of loss for children and parents

The purpose of this section is to look at social and emotional development from birth to adolescence. Human beings are basically social animals, and contrary to previously held beliefs, a neonate (a newborn baby) is not a passive receptor but is an active, social being from the moment of birth. Social and emotional development is a crucial aspect of positive mental health. The way in which the child's emotional well being is promoted will affect his or her ability to develop appropriate social behaviour, including friendships with peers.

Social and emotional development from birth to three years

Although you may not be working with children under three, it is useful to know what developments take place before the child enters the education system. Also, if you are working in the Foundation Stage and encounter a child with significant social and/or emotional difficulties, it might be helpful to be able to match their behaviour to a particular developmental stage in order to plan appropriate intervention. However, the match between a particular aspect of development and the child's chronological age should only be a rough guide, since children develop at different rates.

The table below sets out the main milestones of social and emotional development between birth and three years.

Age	Social/emotional developments observed
Birth to six months	A growing awareness that they are separate individuals and that their behaviour can influence the people around them (for example, making a link between crying and being picked up).
	Will fix on a face and can recognise primary caregivers
	Can indicate distress and pleasure.
	Spontaneous smiling emerges and gradually becomes more discriminatory; i.e. will smile at familiar adults
	Likes being cuddled, will stop crying if picked up
Six to twelve months	Enjoys interactive games such as 'peek a boo'
	Will protest or show distress when separated from primary caregivers
	Responds to name, waves bye bye
	Becomes distressed if a toy is lost or dropped out of reach
	Understands 'no'
	Will give and release objects
Twelve to eighteen months	Can show much more distress if separated from primary caregiver
	Can recognise themself in a mirror or picture
	Begins to imitate
Eighteen months to two years	Able to express a wider range of emotions
	Temper tantrums might emerge
	Will watch other children playing
Two to three years	Temper tantrums much more likely as they experience changes in mood but at the same time find it difficult to regulate their behaviour. Fearfulness can emerge: often at this stage a child will suddenly become afraid of the dark
	Can recognise a range of facial expressions
	Sense of humour emerging, likes to play tricks
	Can be very possessive about toys
	Begins to use 'I' when talking
	Becoming assertive: will refuse to comply with adult requests, shows (and expresses) specific preferences
	Will sometimes be rigid about routines or objects (for example, becomes very attached to a particular toy, or insists on same routine for some activities)
	Will begin to play contentedly if left alone, able to amuse him/herself
	Plays alongside other children
	Children begin to develop a much stronger sense of self and are much more likely to develop opinions about themselves (e.g. by labelling themselves as 'naughty' or 'good')

The foundation stage: three to five years

During the foundation stage years, children gradually develop more interest in each other. The beginnings of co-operation can be seen, in the way each child plays. Sharing is more evident, developing at the same time as cooperative and imaginative play. Children take roles in play and are able to 'act out' situations and everyday events in play. Imagination is very evident in their play. The beginnings of moral understanding can be seen, where children can discriminate between good and bad behaviour and can begin to say what is fair or unfair. At this stage, children begin to discriminate on a gender basis. They are aware of themselves as either female or male and will begin to identify with the parent of the same sex. By the end of the foundation stage, children can appear quite self-sufficient.

Middle and late childhood: six to eleven years

Middle and late childhood sees the growth in awareness of others and a gradual reduction in the egocentricity that characterises early childhood. Children at these stages form closer friendships, tending to have 'best' friends as well as a circle of friends. Friendship groups are usually same sex. The beginnings of empathy can be seen, where children in late childhood will often take an interest in younger children in a caring role. Rules and fairness are dominant features of social development: children gradually develop a strong sense of fairness and it is common to hear 'it's not fair'. Rules are also a feature of play: games can contain complicated rules and rituals and at this stage children begin to take part in organised team games. Children's self-concepts develop and they place importance on their popularity. What their peer group thinks is very important to them!

Adolescence: twelve to sixteen years

The physical changes that occur during adolescence are accompanied by major social and emotional changes. Adolescence is the time when children are become adults, both physically and psychologically. One of the main features of adolescence is the search for identity. The process of changing from child to adult involves developing a clear notion of one's beliefs, values, life goals, occupational and career aspirations. This means that as this process takes place, there is less emotional dependency on parents. We think of teenagers as being rebellious. Conflicts arise as they search for their identity and try to establish their autonomy in a setting where they are still expected to observe rules concerning meal times, cleanliness and returning home at a specified time. These conflicts gradually diminish during later adolescence, as the young person becomes more able to accept the parent's perspective and to take on more adult-orientated activities and also responsibilities in the home, school and community. The peer group is very important to adolescents. They use the peer group as their yardstick to make social comparisons and their support network as a safe setting in which to explore different identities. As well as being physically mature enough to engage in sexual/reproductive behaviour, adolescents develop emotional responses to sexuality, contraception, when to be sexually active, pregnancy and sexually transmitted diseases. Adolescents can believe that they are immune to the consequences of their actions and consequently can engage in risky behaviour which might be related to being sexually active, using drugs, smoking or alcohol abuse.

Summary

This section has outlined the changes that take place in the child's social and emotional development from birth to age sixteen. The process of change over this period sees the child move from emotional dependency on adults, usually the primary caregivers, to an autonomous individual with their own identity, values and beliefs. Along the way, the values and beliefs of significant adults in the child's life influence the development of the autonomous individual. Styles of parenting, therefore, have a significant impact.

Although we associate schools with the pursuit of academic learning, we cannot afford to ignore the social and emotional development of children and young people. One important message from psychology is that academic needs will only be met if social and emotional needs are met first. The psychologist Abraham Maslow proposed this theory. Maslow suggests that our needs form a hierarchy. At the bottom of this hierarchy are our physical needs. These are very basic needs such as the need for food and warmth. Next in the hierarchy are needs related to social and emotional development. These are needs such as belonging, identity, self image and self concept. Needs relating to academic learning go beyond the physical and emotional. Maslow argues that meeting physical and emotional needs is therefore a prerequisite for academic success. This puts a new emphasis on the role of schools and schooling. Whilst we would like to think that schools exist to further academic needs, Maslow's theory suggests that we can only do this successfully if other needs lower down the hierarchy are met. Consequently, we should view schools as catering for a wide range of needs, not just academic. Children and young people who experience some kind of emotional distress or trauma, or who do not have their physical or emotional needs adequately met are less likely to benefit from the academic curriculum.

The next two sections of Part 2 discuss what happens when the child's emotional needs are not met. Theories of attachment help us to understand the importance of close emotional bonds from a very early age, whilst the psychological impact of abuse examines the consequences of damage to the child's emotional development.

Reflection point: social and emotional development

Think about the pupils that you have contact with, and consider the following questions:

■ Do any of them have problems with social and emotional development?

■ What signs do you observe in pupils that lead you to think that their problems are social and/or emotional?

■ What steps does the school take in order to help these pupils?

■ In your day-to-day contact, what do you do?

■ Looking at the developmental stages in this section, when do you draw the line between 'normal' and 'problem' social and emotional development? For example, when does a rebellious adolescent become a problem? Or, when do temper tantrums become a problem?

Attachment

Newborn babies have a surprising range of skills which promote their development. They are attracted to areas of high contrast between black and white. Shortly after birth they will fixate on head-shaped objects painted black and white. They will show almost as much interest in a head-shaped object with features, such as eyes, mouth, noses and hair painted on in random ways as in a similar object with the features painted in the right places. Newborn babies have good hearing and will recognise familiar human voices. They have a good sense of smell and can discriminate the smell of their own mother's milk from that of another woman from at least six days after birth. Hearing and vision are integrated at an early stage. Children as young as one or two months showed distress when they heard their mother's voices coming from a loud speaker placed in a different part of the room from the mother. The importance of early experience is demonstrated through a phenomenon called *imprinting*.

The work of Lorenz looked at the early experiences of a variety of animals. He demonstrated that goslings would treat the first thing that they saw after hatching as their mother. He showed that it was possible for a human to be treated by the goslings as their mother. They would follow Lorenz everywhere and appear to be distressed if they were separated from him. As you might imagine, these experiments were extremely inconvenient for the experimenter! Later versions used brightly coloured Wellington boots. The goslings would treat the boots as their mother, so that different researchers could share the burden of parenting the flock. The goslings learned that the person, or boots, were their prime care givers, only if they saw the person/boots at a certain time after hatching. In other words there was a *critical period* after hatching, when this learning took place. If it did not occur then, it would never occur.

The experiments of Blakemore and Cooper suggested that there are critical times in the development of vision in cats. They raised kittens in a room with only vertical stripes. The kittens wore collars to prevent them seeing their own bodies, so the only things that they saw were vertical lines. Later, the kittens did not respond to horizontal lines and tripped over ropes strung between two chairs. Although these studies were with animals, there is a strong possibility that early infant experiences have an impact on the healthy development of a child.These biologically-programmed behaviours probably developed because they facilitate the conditions needed for successful development. A key element of this is the development of a *bond* between the infant and an adult.

From birth to about eight weeks, babies will react to voices and show some recognition of the faces of familiar adults.

From about two months to seven months infants will demonstrate a clear pre-ference for people. They will complain if they are put down and are more likely to smile at familiar adults than at strangers.

From about seven months to nine months infants begins to show a clear pre-ference for familiar adults. They will show distress if separated from a familiar adult and will show some anxiety to strangers.

From nine months onwards the infant will show attachments to more familiar adults.

Separation anxiety is associated with *bonds*. If an infant is separated from the adult with whom there is an established bond they become distressed. There are different stages:

- protest: the child cries, but can be comforted

- despair: the child stops crying and looking for the adult. They might self-comfort by rocking or thumb sucking

- detachment: the child has given up on the attached adult. When the adult reappears, they may be ignored

Is attachment necessary for healthy development? This question was researched by John Bowlby in the middle of the twentieth century. His starting point was an investigation into the life histories of 88 children who had been referred to a psychiatric clinic. About half of the children had criminal histories. Some of them seemed to lack basic emotions and were described as 'affectionless psycho-paths'. Of these, the vast majority had suffered extensive separations from their mothers. These children had been in foster homes and hospitals and had little contact with their birth families. The children who displayed emotions had not experienced these periods of separation.

This idea was explored with monkeys by Harlow. He used rhesus monkeys and separated the monkeys from their mothers shortly after birth. He was testing an idea suggested by behavioural psychologists, that infants liked mothers because they were fed by them. The monkeys were provided with two surrogate mothers. One was made of wire, but contained a bottle with milk; the other was made of soft cloth and looked like an adult monkey. The baby monkeys spent most of their time clinging to the surrogate monkey that looked and felt like the mother. They would transfer to the wire surrogate just to feed. When the monkeys were disturbed by a researcher cleaning the cage, the baby monkeys would cling to the surrogate monkey, not the wire one.

Bowlby developed a theory that a child needs to bond with their mother to promote healthy social development. Children who fail to bond with their mothers were destined to miserable and affectionless lives. However, this view was challenged. The evidence that there was a group of children who had been separated from their mothers and showed no emotion did not prove that one event caused the other. The sample of cases was not typical of the population as a whole. It was possible that a third factor was responsible for both the separation and the lack of emotion.

Do attachment figures have to be the natural parents of the child? This question has been the subject of much research. Other cultures have different family systems. A radical experiment in alternative ways of rearing children operates in Israel, where Kibbutz communities have been established. Childcare, along with everything else, is shared. Children are raised not in small family units but by teams of adults who work in the children's house. When the children were tested for attachment to adults, they demonstrated that they were attached to both their natural parents *and* the adults working in the children's house. Within the UK there was concern that the using day nurseries for children might have a negative impact on development. Various studies have covered day nurseries, child minders and use of *au pairs* or other adults who look after children in the family home. The overall conclusions were that the single most important factor was the *quality* of interaction between the child and the adults. When children were left alone, or encouraged to be quiet, their development was less successful. The important factors are that children are talked to, played with and involved in joint activities with adults.

Families

The context of the early relationships between children and adults is usually the *family*. Families are found in a wide range of species. The family offers protection and stability, which are required for quality attachments to form. However, families take different forms in different cultures and have changed over the last generation. The increase of reconstituted families following parental separation is of particular importance.

Research into the influence of parental separation on children has looked at four different groups:

- children from families which are intact and with low discord

- children from families which are intact, but with high family discord

- children from families which have separated and then reconstituted with one parent or step parents (one reconstitution)

- children from families which have separated and reconstituted more than once.

The findings suggest that the lower down the list the family is, the more negative influences to self-image, social life, school work, behaviour and health occur. The disturbing finding is that children from families with significant disagreements and discord do better than those from separated and reconstituted families. We must therefore conclude that the presence of both parents is positive, even if they spend a lot of their time disagreeing. The significant factor seems to be how many times children's family lives are disrupted.

Loss

There are a variety of ways in which loss can be a part of the lives of children:

- departure or death of a parent or other family member

- departure or death of a child

- discovery of some difference in a child such as disability

This last group is important to understand. Many teaching assistants support children with some developmental difference. The processes surrounding the discovery of these differences are similar to those of bereavement.

There are similarities in the processes of loss. In fact the term *bereavement* has an Anglo-Saxon root. The old word *beriafen* means to be robbed. In all known human societies there are processes around death.

The processes of grief appear to manifest in stages:

1. numbness – the reality of the loss is not appreciated, everything appears unreal, there is an emptiness, bewilderment and sense of not being able to cope there may be panic attacks and the individual may be restless and need to do things

2. yearning and searching – there is an urge to recover the lost person, the sense of yearning may come over the individual in waves over time, there will be crying and a sense of anger, we ask 'Why?'

3. disorganisation and despair – the loss is accepted, attempts to recover the lost person are abandoned, this can be experienced as aimlessness and apathy, people may feel depressed, a reorganisation of the sense of self without the lost person is begun

4. reorganisation and adjustment – new behaviours and habits emerge, a new image of self without the lost person is created, beliefs associated with the lost person are replaced by new attitudes and behaviours.

Not all people go through the stages of grief in a smooth manner. The psycho-therapist Lindemann, describes nine types of distortions to the above processes:

■ overactivity without a sense of loss, but with an increased sense of well-being and zest for life

■ development of symptoms similar to those experienced by the deceased

■ development of a medical illness

■ changes to relationships with family and friends leading to social isolation

■ fury and anger towards specific people

■ a restriction of anger so that the individual appears emotionally cold and distant

■ loss of initiative and ability to make decisions

■ new behaviours such as spending sprees and discarding friends

■ depression, insomnia, agitation, guilt, worthlessness and potential suicide. (Lindemann, 1944)

When a child is born with some kind of disability, many parents undergo psychological processes similar to bereavement. Although a death has not occurred, parents-to-be prepare themselves for a new child. They make plans, have hopes and aspirations for themselves and the newborn child. There is an assumption that the child will grow up to be independent of their parents. The family continues through the new children. The discovery of a disability can destroy all of these plans. The parents are grieving the child they expected to have. These stages can be described as:

Stage 1 Shock
This is the numbness described earlier. There is a sense of unreality, bewilderment and fear. There may be a tremendous amount of infor-mation offered. Little can be taken in.

Stage 2 Denial/Anger
This is similar to the yearning and questioning stage. Very often there will be a lot of new information given shortly after the discovery. This can lead to information overload. Parents cannot take in all of the advice and services being offered.

Stage 3 Guilt/Questions/Confusion
Parents may feel guilty. Ideas may arise that the disability was as a result of something that they did wrong, or some aspect of their family history that was not considered. Some conditions are genetically linked. (*Duchene muscular dystrophy* is carried by women, but expressed in boys.)

Stage 4 Adjustment
This is often not total. Parents may remain aggressive. Such aggression can be expressed towards professionals (doctors, therapists, psychologists etc). It can lead to unrealistic expectations for the child (my child *will* walk/talk). It can lead to fears of isolation for themselves and their child. (What will happen after we're dead and gone?) It can also lead to acceptance. (This is what life is going to be like for me and my child) Acceptance can, include a realisation that they are unable or unwilling to care for the child.

Stage 5 Stability
If the parent remains the prime care-giver for the child, there can be a sense of assertiveness or mission (I will run a support group/charity for this condition). However some parents may actually reject the child. The child will be cared for by others. (Arnold, Boucher, McRobert and Rimmer, 2001)

We present these stages in this order, but parents and families can move from one stage to another and back again. There is a degree of fluidity between stages two and five.

The implications for teaching assistants can be considerable. Parents may have considerable needs to talk and be listened to. Often the teaching assistant is an easy person to access. Parents can spend considerable periods of time talking. It can be tempting to suggest that the parents are 'simply neurotic' or 'obsessed'. It might be more helpful to think that the parents are working through the stages of grief for the child they wished they'd had. Sympathetic listening and non-judgmental acceptance of their need to be listened to is a great help to the bereaved parent.

References and further reading

Arnold, C Boucher, L McRobert, R and Rimmer S (2001) *Supporting Children with Physical Needs*. Walsall LEA and Walsall Health Trust, Unpublished course for teaching assistants

Lindemann E (1944) 'The Symptomatology and Management of Acute Grief.' *American Journal of Psychiatry* 101:141

Maslow A H (1943) A theory of human motivation. *Psychological Review,* 50, 370-396

6

The Psychological Impact
of Child Abuse

This chapter

- examines the phenomenon of child abuse

- describes the signs and symptoms of child abuse

- describes the long term effects of child abuse

- describes ways and means of assisting abused children

In the eyes of most of us, children are to be loved, cherished and protected. The idea of harming children is abhorrent. Yet the incidence of child abuse is alarmingly high. How does psychology help our understanding of both the behaviour itself and ways of preventing its damage?

As with other areas, the different psychological approaches offer different insights into this area:

- The behavioural school considers that the perpetrator of the abuse receives some satisfaction from the acts. In other words, abusers are rewarded for their acts. The rewards may come from a sense of intimacy with the victim or a sense of power. For the victim s/he may be fearful that disclosing the facts of the abuse may have significant negative consequences, the break up of the family or further abuse by the perpetrator.

- The social constructionist dimension reminds us that the concept of abuse is one that is created by people living in a society with norms and rules. What might once have been normal practice can be thought of quite a differently. The Reverend William Cooper wrote an account of the history of the rod (cane) in 1876 and found:

> It is recorded of a Suabian schoolmaster that during his fifty-one years superintendence of a large school he had given 911,500 canings, 121,000 floggings, 136,000 tips with the ruler, 10,200 boxes on the ear and 22,700 tasks by heart. It was further calculated that he had made 700 boys stand on peas, 6,000 kneel on a sharp piece of wood, 5,000 wear the fool's-cap and 1,700 hold the rod. (Cooper, 1876)

This was not considered abusive at the time. Possibly only the 'tasks by heart' would not attract a criminal charge today. Within families, what is considered to be abuse may differ. A study published in the 1960s describes the huge variation in practices in families when toilet training children. There are descriptions of children being hit with a belt, shamed, shouted at, and smacked if they wet the bed:

> Tell her she's a dirty little madam. I slap her if she's awake. (quoted in Newson and Newson, 1968)

> I shout at him, and I threaten to hit him; but I never do. When I take him to bed, I say 'Do you want to use a pot?' He says 'No', and I say 'You wet that bed! Let me find that bed wet in the morning and see what you'll get! (in Newson and Newson, 1968)

Other families taught by praising success:

> Well actually he's very proud of his tie, and I say 'When you don't wet the bed, you'll be a big boy and you'll be able to have another tie, so that, like Daddy, you'll be able to have one hanging in the wardrobe and one to wear'. (in Newson and Newson, 1968)

What is considered normal in one family might be considered abusive by another.

■ The psychodynamic school offers a unique insight. This school considers that motives and drives exist of which we are unaware. Abuse can be seen as a process of unconscious communication. The victim of abuse can be thought of as an object made up to represent a part of the abuser's self. If an abuser has been hurt in childhood, they can create something that they can hurt in turn. If an adult has survived abuse and finds themselves humiliated or hurt again, the experience of that pain can trigger memories of childhood which, in turn, can lead the individual to hurt someone else. The victim can become the receptacle for the abuser's pain. If the victim refuses to take this role, the relationship can break down. In the case of adults, they might separate. For children, this option is rarely available.

Sexual abuse

There are a number of different ways of defining and describing child sexual abuse. One is:

> A child (anyone under sixteen) is sexually abused when another person who is sexually mature, involves the child in any activity which the other person expects to lead to their sexual arousal. (Baker and Duncan, 1985)

Estimates of the prevalence of sexual abuse vary, but make for disturbing reading. A survey of studies carried out in North America suggest that for girls, the figure is between 6 per cent and 62 per cent, whilst for boys it is between 3 per cent and 16 per cent. The surveys are particularly difficult to conduct and the wide range in findings reflects those difficulties. One study found that 16 per cent of girls had been involved in incest abuse before the age of eighteen. It found that 31 per cent of girls had been subject to abuse from non-family members. The total number was 38 per cent. Thus over one third of women in this study reported some kind of sexual abuse during childhood.

Signs and symptoms

Glaser and Frosh (1993) have described the following signs (si) and symptoms (sy). The key to symbols is as follows: si = sign; sy = symptom; * = supportive of diagnosis of child sexual abuse. (*) = a learnt pattern. The lack of * indicated a non-specific but possible alerting sign.

Aspect of abuse and its *physical* manifestation:

1. **Trauma**
   - vaginal bleeding in pre-pubertal girls * (sy)
   - genital laceration * (si)
   - bruising in genital area * (si)
   - enlarged vaginal opening, scarred hymen * (si)
   - vaginal discharge (sy, si)
   - vulvovaginal soreness or discomfort (si)
   - anal laceration of scarring * (si)
   - lax or pouting anus * (si)
   - reflex anal dilation greater than 1cm * (si)
   - acute and chronic anal verge changes including fissures * (si)
   - rectal bleeding (sy)
   - faecal soiling or retention (sy)
   - discomfort on mictuation and recurrent urinary tract infections (si, sy)
   - evidence of non-accidental injury or neglect (si)

2. Infection
- sexually transmitted disease including genital warts (*) (sy, si)
- vaginal discharge (sy)

3. Sexual intercourse
- pregnancy (particularly when identity of father is uncertain (*) (sy, si)

Aspect of abuse and *emotional and behavioural* manifestation:

1. premature and inappropriate sexualisation

- explicit or frequent sexual preoccupation in talk and play (*) (si)
- sexualisation of relationships * (si)
- inappropriate involvement of younger children in sexual activity *
- premature sexual awareness (*) (si)
- undue avoidance of men * (si)
- excessive masturbation (si)

2. Experiences of guilt, confusion, anxiety, fear or anger
- hints of possession of secrets * (sy)
- running away from home * (sy)
- parasuicide * (sy)
- child psychiatric problems (sy, si)
- educational underachievement (si)
- adolescent depression (si)

3. Family relationship patterns
- other sexually abused children in the family *
- known contact with sexual abuser *
- distant mother-child relationship
- unclear intergenerational boundaries
- other form of child abuse in family
- parental alcohol abuse

The initial effects of sexual abuse have been described under four headings:

■ **Traumatic sexualisation**
The child's sexuality is shaped in a developmentally inappropriate way. Children can be rewarded (given sweets, treats etc) for sexual acts with the abuser. Frightening memories can be associated with sexual acts. Children who have been traumatised by sexual experiences can develop peculiar sexualised behaviours. They can be confused about socially acceptable boundaries of sexualised behaviour.

■ **Betrayal**
Children are abused by people they trust, such as fathers. The abuse can be silently condoned by other family members. Mothers fail to protect

their children from abusing fathers. When abused children tell an adult about the abuse, they are disbelieved. This leads to a sense of betrayal and lack of trust in adults.

▪ **Powerlessness**
Victims are subjected to repeated abuse. They cannot avoid it so they submit. They are unable to end the abuse.

▪ **Stigmatisation**
Children feel guilty, ashamed and bad. 'If I had been a good person, this would never have happened.', 'What must I have done to deserve this?' are thoughts in the heads of the victim. Stigmatisation can come from the knowledge that the child has. This behaviour is not accepted in our society. I must keep it secret. Additionally, the victim can be stigmatised by others. If disclosed, others can blame the child, justifying the attitude by suggesting that the child led the abuser on, or that the child is now, somehow spoiled goods.

What follows is a more detailed list describing the dynamics (how the abuser/victim interact), psychological impact and behavioural manifestations (observable features) relating to each of the four aspects of child sexual abuse.

1. Traumatic Sexualisation

Dynamics
- child rewarded for sexual behaviour inappropriate to developmental level
- offender exchanges attention for sex
- sexual parts of child fetishised
- offender transmits misconceptions about sexual behaviour and sexual morality
- conditioning of sexual activity with negative emotions and memories

Psychological impact
- increased salience of sexual issues
- confusion about sexual identity
- confusion about sexual norms
- confusion of sex with love and care-getting or care-giving
- negative associations to sexual activities and arousal sensations
- aversion to sex or intimacy

Behavioural manifestations
- sexual preoccupations and compulsive sexual behaviours
- precocious sexual activity
- aggressive sexual behaviours
- promiscuity

- prostitution
- sexual dysfunctions; flashbacks; difficulty in arousal and orgasm
- avoidance of or phobic reactions to sexual intimacy
- inappropriate sexualisation of parenting

2. Stigmatisation
Dynamics
- offender blames and disparages the victim
- offender and others pressure child for secrecy
- child infers attitudes of shame about activities
- others have shocked reaction to disclosure
- others blame child for events
- victim is stereotyped as damaged goods

Psychological impact
- guilt, shame
- lowered self-esteem
- sense of difference from others

Behavioural manifestations
- isolation
- drug or alcohol abuse
- criminal involvement
- self-mutilation
- suicide

3. Betrayal
Dynamics
- trust and vulnerability manipulated
- violation of expectation that others will provide care and protection
- child's well-being disregarded
- lack of support and protection from parent(s)

Psychological impact
- grief, depression
- extreme dependency
- impaired ability to judge trustworthiness of others
- mistrust, especially of men
- anger, hostility

Behavioural manifestations
- clinging
- vulnerability to subsequent abuse and exploitation
- allowing own children to be victimised
- isolation

- discomfort in intimate relationships
- marital problems
- aggressive behaviour
- delinquency

4. Powerlessness

Dynamics
- body territory invaded against the child's wishes
- vulnerability to invasion continues over time
- offender uses force or trickery to involve child
- child feels unable to protect self and halt abuse
- repeated experience of fear
- child is unable to make others believe

Psychological impact
- anxiety, fear
- lowered sense of efficacy
- perception of self as victim
- need to control
- identification with the aggressor

Behavioural manifestations
- nightmares
- phobias
- somatic complaints; eating and sleeping disorders
- depression
- dissociation
- running away
- school problems, truancy
- employment problems
- vulnerability to subsequent victimisation
- aggressive behaviour, bullying
- delinquency
- becoming an abuser

(Finkelhorn and Browne, 1986)

Long term effects can include:

- aversion to sex
- flashbacks
- difficulties with sexual arousal
- negative attitudes towards sexuality
- guilt and shame
- betrayal and anger leading to antisocial behaviour and delinquency

- eating disorders
- bullying others
- depression

(Baker and Duncan, 1985)

It is important for teaching assistants to be aware of these features of sexual abuse. Teaching assistants are usually in a better position than teachers to notice the signs.

Physical abuse

The signs of physical abuse are usually clear. Explanations of bruises, broken bones, swelling and even bite marks need to be carefully considered, but many medical practitioners consider that judgements are much easier than those made about sexual or emotional abuse.

The following is a list of injuries which arouse suspicion:

- bruises and abrasions on faces of young babies (especially those too young to sit up)

- damage or injury around or inside the mouth

- repeated and numerous bruises on the heads of toddlers

- bruising or swelling of the skin that has occurred more than once

- two similar injuries (eg two bruised eyes)

- fingertip bruises to the front or back of chest, arms or face

- bruises to back of legs, buttocks, back, mouth, cheeks, behind ears, stomach, chest, under arm, genital area, rectal area and neck

- bites that are oval or crescent-shaped and greater than three cm across they have been caused by adults or children with adult teeth

* burns and scalds on one area of the body

* fractures

* neurological damage – although this is difficult to observe

Emotional abuse

To understand the way we see emotional abuse it is necessary to have a shared understanding of what a child's basic needs are from adults. This enables us to look at situations in which these needs are not met. These are the situations we can describe as being emotionally abusive for children. One list of emotional needs of children was provided by Kelmer Pringle in 1974. They are:

- physical care and protection
- affection and approval
- stimulation and teaching
- discipline and control appropriate to the child's age
- opportunity and encouragement to develop independence and self reliance

Emotional abuse is considered to be present when the above needs are lacking. It implies rejection of the child's needs. This might be seen when parents withhold approval, love and attention. It can also be present if parents punish normal behaviour such as walking, smiling, exploration and talking.

The impact of emotional abuse can include:

- impaired physical development
- poor attachment and bonding
- impaired or delayed cognitive development such as speech
- poor functioning in nurseries and play groups, eg cooperative play
- difficulties in forming and maintaining relationships with adults and peers

The lack of physical evidence of emotional abuse makes it the hardest to prove.

Long term impacts of abuse

Earlier in this chapter we discussed attachment and grief. Recent studies of people in the youth justice system support earlier findings that children who fail to become firmly attached to adults, or who are the victims of abuse, are more likely to get into trouble with the law. However, we must take care when considering findings of this nature. Studies which start from examination of people with difficulties but do not systematically compare with other groups, are not always reliable. Consider the following. Imagine a researcher interested in the incidence and cause of depression. The researcher asks numerous questions, including items about attendance at church. The researcher finds that 95 per cent of depressed people did not attend church and concludes that there is a link between church non-attendance and depression. Can you see the mistake the researcher has made? If the researcher does not compare these findings from depressed people with those from a non-depressed sample, you cannot draw that particular conclusion. If it turned out that 95 per cent of the whole population did not attend church anyway, there would be no difference between the groups. Even if there was a difference (eg in the depressed sample only 5 per cent went to church, compared with 10 per cent of the non-depressed group) the research needs to demonstrate that one *causes* the other. Simply finding a statistical link does not reveal the cause.

However, some findings are interesting. In a major study in the 1990s by Boswell, over 90 per cent of young people in the youth justice system had a history of grief, loss or abuse. A project in Falkirk examined families of persistent offenders. They looked at:

- death of a parent or carer
- rejection by one or both parents, or carers, including neglect
- divorce or separation of parents
- continual change in residence
- loss of parent due to serious mental or physical illness
- significant loss of status in family due to step parent arrangement

In a study in Greater Manchester, 147 files were selected from those of 1,027 known to the Youth Offending Team (YOT). They looked at the first five factors listed above. In 46 per cent of the cases at least two factors were present, and 92 per cent had at least one.

Implications included high drug use and problems in expressing emotions, such as anger, in socially acceptable ways. It can be suggested that use of drugs is a strategy for coping with the sense of loss. There is a strong link between street crime and drug use.

However the figures are examined, it is clear that not all children who experienced these traumas ended up in the youth justice system. Some children seemed to be more *resilient* than others. Resilience is becoming an area of interest for psychologists and social workers.

A study undertaken in Salford found that resilient children had three sources:

1. I have
- people around me I trust and love me, no matter what
- people who set limits for me so I know when to stop before there is danger of trouble
- people who show me how to do things right by the way they do things
- people who want me to learn to do things on my own
- people who help me when I am sick, in danger or need to learn

2. I am
- a person people can like and love
- glad to do nice things for others and show my concern
* respectful of myself and others
* willing to be responsible for what I do
* sure things will be alright

3. I can

- talk to others about things that frighten or bother me.
- find ways to solve problems I face.
- control myself when I feel like doing something not right or dangerous.
- figure out when it is a good time to talk to someone or take action.
- find someone to help me when I need it.

(Allen, Kyng and Springings, 2003)

So are negative outcomes of child abuse inevitable? Psychology offers some hope that this might not necessarily be so.

The team in Salford are using these ideas to build programmes to increase resilience in vulnerable young people. Other approaches have included behavioural psychology which developed *aversion therapy* during which abusers were shown pictures of abusive scenes and given electric shocks, in an attempt to teach the abusers to associate abuse with the shock. *Social constructionist* psychology uses high-profile public messages which describe what abuse is and invite victims and those aware of abusive situations to bring the abuse to the attention of relevant authorities. Psychodynamic psychology offers long term therapy for both the abuser and the victim. This chapter concludes with ideas from this approach. The therapist Alice Miller has described a framework for understanding and helping both abusers and victims.

She suggests that all children need to grow, develop, love and to express their needs and feelings for self-protection. Children need adults to respect, love and protect them so that they may become well-adjusted adults. If these basic needs are not met and children are abused in order to gratify unmet needs in adults, then the children will not grow into well-adjusted adults. The effects can be long-lasting. The normal reactions to being abused are to feel anger and pain. However some children are not allowed to express their anger. This results in them suppressing their feelings, repressing memories of the trauma and even idealising the perpetrators of the abuse. Some children may direct their feelings of anger back on themselves and turn to destructive acts against others such as criminal behaviour, or against themselves by using drugs and alcohol, or by falling into prostitution, depression or suicide. If these people become parents they can take revenge on their own children. Parents who hit children do so to avoid the painful memories associated with their own childhood. For abused children to develop into healthy adults, it is essential that they come into contact with at least one adult who can communicate to them that it was the environment, not the child, that led to the abuse. Abused children often blame themselves for the abuse. Adults can see children as dominated by wicked drives, leading them in to craftiness. This is not the case. Even the most confusing behaviour becomes clear when the abuse is understood.

She ends with a noble thought:

> People whose integrity has not been damaged in childhood, who were protected, respected and treated honestly by their parents, will be – both in their youth and adulthood – intelligent, responsive, empathic, and highly sensitive. They will take pleasure in life and will not feel any need to kill or even hurt others or themselves. They will use their power to defend themselves but not attack others. They will not be able to do otherwise than to respect and protect those weaker than themselves, including their children, because this is what they have learned from their own experience and because it is this knowledge (and not the experience of cruelty) that had been stored up inside them from the beginning. Such people will be incapable of understanding why earlier generations had to build up a gigantic war industry in order to feel at ease and safe from the world. Since it will not have to be their unconscious life-task to ward off intimidation experienced at a very early age, they will be able to deal with attempts at intimidation in their adult life more rationally and more creatively. (Miller, 2000)

Whilst some other psychologists may disagree with the theory, most would support the positive message described.

References and further reading

Allen, C Kyng, E and Springings, N. (2003) *Street Crime and Drug Use in Greater Manchester.* Youth Justice Trust

Baker, A and Duncan, S (1985) Child Sexual Abuse: A Study of Prevalence in Great Britain. *Child Abuse and Neglect* 9, pp 457-67

Boswell, G (1996) in *Just Briefs* (September 2003) Youth Justice Trust

Cooper, W (1876) in Menninger, K (1930) *The Human Mind.* Toronto, Longmans Green and Company

Finkelhorn, D and Browne, A (1986) *A Source Book on Child Abuse.* London, Sage

Glaser, D and Frosh, S (1993) *Child Sexual Abuse.* Basingstoke, Macmillan

Miller, A (2000) in Itzin, C. *Home Truths about Child Sexual Abuse.* London, Routlege

Newson, J and Newson, E (1963) *Patterns of Infant Care in an Urban Community.* Pelican Books, Harmondworth

Part 3
The Psychology of Learning

7

Models of Learning

This chapter

■ presents a range of theories about how individuals learn

■ examines these theories with reference to learning in educational settings

■ applies these theories to the role of the teaching assistant

Introduction to Part 3

How do we learn? Why do some children (and adults!) fail to learn, or find it difficult to learn? How does knowledge about learning help us to know how to teach? These questions are fundamental to our understanding of schools and schooling.

Psychology can tell us a great deal about learning. Indeed, we could devote an entire book just to this aspect of psychology! The various schools of psychology all have views about what constitutes learning and the reasons for failure or difficulties in relation to the process of learning. All the schools of psychology have a range of convenience. This is true of this section. In considering a variety of theories about learning, we will consider ranges of convenience in relation to school learning. This is not to say that any one theory or view is better than another, only that a particular view might be more relevant to learning in school than others. Working through this section should provide a better understanding of learning, which will improve your professional practice.

Can we begin with a definition of learning?

As there are a number of theories about learning, and each has its own particular definition of what is meant by learning. One thing that all the theories do have in common is the view that learning involves some kind of change. Common sense tells us that after we have learned something we have changed in some way. For example we add to our repertoire of facts about something that interests us, or we are able to perform a skill, such as driving or knitting, that we couldn't do before. The various schools of psychology will all have a different view of the type and nature of the change that takes place as a result of learning.

How Part 3 of this book is organised

The purpose of Part 3 is therefore to present a range of views about learning. Each view is accompanied by one or more practical applications that you may meet in schools. In order to bring some coherence into this vast area of psychology, different theories about learning have been categorised into seven *dimensions*. The theories of learning associated with each dimension emphasise a particular perspective about learning. The dimensions and their emphases are as follows:

- *Biological*: the role of neurology
- *Behavioural*: the role of behaviour
- *Instructional*: the role of instruction
- *Social constructivist*: the role of social contexts and interaction
- *Experiential*: the role of experience
- *Intelligence*: the role of IQ and intelligence

Introducing Jennifer

A case study is used so as to help you relate these theories of learning to your work in school.

Jennifer is a fictional pupil who has learning difficulties. Below is a brief pen portrait of her. At the end of each section in Part 3, Jennifer's difficulties are examined in the relation to the views of learning emphasised by each particular dimension. At the end of Part 3, the case study will be used to reflect on the different views of learning that have been discussed.

Jennifer is in a Year 4 class of a mainstream primary school and is aged nine years and two months. She has attended this school since nursery. She lives at home with her mum and dad and has a brother and a sister. Jennifer is the middle child in the family. Her older sister attends the local secondary school. Her younger brother has just started at Jennifer's school and is in the reception class.

Jennifer was always slower than the other children to pick things up. In nursery, her language skills were noticeably poorer than her peers, although she was talkative. Throughout infant school, she was much slower than her peers to acquire the basics of reading and writing and in the Key Stage 2 SATS she was Level W for all the core subjects. This prompted school to place her on the SEN register. She continued to struggle when she moved into junior school. In recent assessment, she had a reading age below six (she didn't score on the test). She can read twenty words from the NLS Reception List of high frequency words and can spell fifteen of these words. She recognises letter sounds but can't yet blend sounds together consistently or fluently. When she is reading, she often spells out each individual letter of an unfamiliar word but then can't read the word. Often she's not aware that her reading errors don't make sense. She can write her name but finds it very difficult to write anything else independently. In free writing, the teaching assistant writes down what Jennifer dictates. She can count to fifty but doesn't seem to understand place value. She can add and subtract up to and within ten and can recognise some coins. She takes her reading book home and her mum hears her read, but they are both feeling frustrated because Jennifer has been bringing the same book home for weeks now and she still can't read it properly. Her mum finds it difficult to know how to help as she doesn't read that well herself.

Jennifer is never any bother; she's enthusiastic about school and always tries her best. Sometimes she's a bit over enthusiastic, tending to 'jump in' with an answer before she's thought about it properly. She also tends not to remember things from one day or week to the next. One day she will read all her flashcards correctly, then the next day she looks blank as if she's never seen the words before! Her mum took her for a hearing and sight test but no problems were detected. Her class teacher has teaching assistant support every morning. The teaching assistant usually works with small groups of children within the class. Jennifer is always included in this small group work. Jennifer has an Individual Education Plan (IEP) that helps to focus the work of the teaching assistant. The IEP contains targets related to literacy and numeracy.

The biological dimension

A biological perspective on learning would emphasise that the changes that take place as a result of learning are related to neurological factors. Conversely, learning difficulties would be attributed to neurological defects or deficiencies. Our starting point, therefore, is to consider some basic information about the way in which the human brain works.

The structure and function of the brain

The brain is made up of two main types of cells: neurones and glial cells. Neurones are the brain's communicators. They receive, store and transmit information. Neurones come in many shapes and sizes, depending on the function that they serve. For example, some neurones receive and transmit information related to our senses, whilst others receive and transmit information related to our physical movement (motor skills). Glial cells play a supporting role in order to help the neurones do their job (for example, by being an extra energy supply).

Neurones work by communicating with each other. This is a chemical and electrical process that takes place within the brain. Messages are sent and received via the part of the neurone called the axon. The electrical message is then changed to a chemical message and relayed across the synapse (or space between neurones). These chemicals are called neurotransmitters. Neurotransmitters affect our behaviour patterns. Serotonin is a neurotransmitter that can play a part in depression. Some drugs used to treat depression are designed to affect serotonin levels in the brain.

The brain can be divided into three main areas:

The lower brain: This part of the brain controls our survival systems. For example, when we are confronted by a threat, the 'flight or fight' mechanism is triggered. The body receives a surge of adrenaline in order to prepare us to either confront or retreat from the situation. This mechanism, and the physiological change that accompanies it, is controlled by the lower brain. Other functions, such as breathing, are controlled by this area of the brain. This part of the brain is sometimes called the 'reptilian brain' since it is similar in structure and function to the brains of reptiles and is the most primitive part of our brain.

The limbic system: This part of the brain controls emotions and memory. It is sometimes referred to as the 'mid brain' as it is located between the lower brain and the cerebral cortex.

The cerebral cortex: All animals have a brain. The major difference between the brains of humans and other species is that humans have the most highly developed cerebral cortex. This part of the brain is where higher order processes take place. It is also called the *neocortex*. The cerebral cortex is separated into two halves: the left and right hemispheres. The hemispheres are connected by the *corpus callosum*. Each hemisphere controls the opposite side of our bodies: the right hemisphere controls the left side of our body and the left hemisphere controls the right side. The cerebral cortex is divided into four main areas, or lobes. Each lobe is associated with different aspects of our thinking or functioning. The lobes are:

The frontal lobes: As the name implies, this is the front part of our brain. It is associated with planning and decision making. Aspects of personality and behaviour are thought to be associated with the frontal lobe. The frontal lobe also controls our motor coordination, in relation to voluntary and skilled motor movements.

The parietal lobes: Associated with spatial awareness and understanding of language.

The temporal lobes: Associated with processing sound, with emotion and with aspects of speech and language.

The occipital lobes: Associated with processing visual information

Memory

Memory is a crucial element of successful learning. It is included in this section since our brains are involved in the processes of remembering and forgetting. Certain parts of the brain are associated specifically with memory. A basic view of how memory works is to liken it to a storage system. Our brain stores information on a short term and long term basis (you might have heard the terms *short term memory* and *long term memory*. From a purely biological point of view, memory involves changes in our neural structure as information is processed, stored and then retrieved when required.

Models of the way in which memory works were influenced by the development of computer technology, where very large amounts of information could be processed and analysed electronically. These models of memory developed from the 1950s onwards, as the discipline of computer science became more sophisticated and was brought to the attention of a wider audience. These models are known as *multi-store* models. Many psychologists found the multi-store models too simple, so other models were suggested. For example, Baddeley proposes a *working memory* model, suggesting that our short term memory has three main elements: central executive (related to attention), articulatory loop (related to holding information as speech) and visuo spatial (related to holding information visually and spatially). Other researchers suggest that there are a larger range of ways of storing information. For example, Perfetti (1979) suggests that there are seven levels of processing information: acoustic, syntactic, semantic, referential, thematic and functional.

Although there are many different ways of representing the process of memory, what is clear is that this process involves processing, storage and retrieval. The way in which these three main aspects of memory work is reflected in the variety of models of memory, which suggest that we might process and remember in different ways: we have an *auditory* memory and a *visual* memory. Important points from the memory models that might be relevant to learning in school are summarised as follows:

- transfer from short-term to long-term memory is related to the amount of rehearsal

- imagery plays a part in memory. For example, it is easier to remember a list of nouns that we can represent visually, such as cat, house or television than a list of nouns that are labels for abstract concepts such as justice or happiness

- we use mnemonics when we remember. A *mnemonic* is a device we use to aid memory. An example might be the way in which we remember the colours of the rainbow:

Richard **Of** York **G**ave **B**attle **I**n **V**ain

The initial letter is the prompt to remember the colours: red, orange, yellow, green, blue, indigo, violet.

Categorising helps us to remember. An efficient way of processing information is to put it into categories. For example, if I know that the category 'dog' will include animals that have four legs, a tail and can bark, when I see a picture or meet a new example, I don't have to worry about describing its features or even knowing its breed as I can file it away under 'dog'. This aspect of memory is called *semantic memory*. Part of this model of memory is an emphasis on concept development. A concept is defined as a class or set into which we can place units of information. Some examples of concepts are: time concepts (now, later), quantity concepts (more, less) or size concepts (big, small). In these examples, there are superordinate concepts (time, quantity, size) that subdivide further into other related concepts.

Activity: thinking about memory in relation to your work in school

How many times have you heard (or said) the following: 'he doesn't remember anything from one minute/hour/day/week to the next'? This activity might help you to address the problems that lead to such a statement.

- ■ summarise the key factors that play a part in retention

- ■ then take an example of something you are working on with a pupil in class where retention is a concern

- ■ now take each key factor and work it into your teaching plan for this child

An example might be learning spellings. One of the ways that you might help the pupil to memorise is to present the words in families or categories: that is, the words learned use the same letter patterns (for example, **night**, **right**, **fight**)

Practical applications of the biological model: brain based learning and accelerated learning

Brain-based learning emphasises that we should take account of how the brain works in order to learn effectively. Brain-based learning is an example of the way in which a biological framework influences the way in which learning is organised and delivered. Brain-based learning has fifteen core principles and there are examples of the way in which these principles are translated into practical learning experiences. A classroom utilising brain-based learning would have a specially designed area for group learning and would make use of music as a means of enhancing learning. Background music of a certain type is thought to make pupils more receptive. Brain-based learning uses three main methods

- orchestrated immersion, which means being immersed fully in the learning experience. For example, if a class was following a project about the Tudors, the whole classroom would be made into a Tudor house or palace

- relaxed alertness which means that the learner can be challenged in a fear free context

- active processing which means that the learner consolidates and inter-nalises learning. This is done by making connections to prior learning.

Accelerated Learning is based on Gardner's theory of multiple intelligences. It is included as an example of the way in which a biological approach to learning is applied because it is based on the notion that learning tries to activate the lower brain. The reason for this is that this part of the brain is concerned with our automatic functions, things that we do without having to think about them, such as breathing. Therefore, if we can direct learning techniques to activate this part of the brain, then learning will take place automatically and seemingly effortlessly. Accelerated Learning is an approach that brings together a number of techniques associated with brain-based learning. For example, it uses music in order to affect mood and receptiveness. Brain Gym is another aspect of Accelerated Learning. It aims to balance interaction between the left and right hemispheres of the brain and is a series of physical movements designed to achieve this equilibrium.

Dyslexia: an example of the neurological dimension in a debate about learning difficulties

Advances in the technology associated with neurology have contributed to the field of education. It is possible to identify specific areas of the brain that are associated with specific activities such as reading. It is possible to detect activity in specific areas of the brain when an individual is reading words, or doing phonological processing tasks that involve manipulation of sounds.

Dyslexia is an aspect of difficulty that has embraced advances in neurology. A definition of dyslexia almost always implies that the child's difficulties with some aspect of literacy are specific in nature. That is, the child only experiences difficulties with very specific aspects of literacy but his or her attainment in all other curriculum areas is considered to be average or above. This definition is in contrast to a child thought to have non-specific literacy difficulties, where the problems experienced by this pupil with reading, writing or spelling are part of low attainment across the board in all areas of the curriculum.

Dyslexia has been highlighted in this section about biological approaches to learning, because it is a good example of some of the circular arguments that ensue when we begin to look for neurological reasons for learning difficulties. As we said earlier, there is a distinction made between poor readers who are dyslexic and non-dyslexic. Behind this distinction is the notion of the role of intelligence: that dyslexic pupils are of average or above average intelligence and that their reading difficulties cannot be attributed to low intelligence. To support this theory, neurology has been involved in the search for the cause of dyslexia.

Research has been carried out involving various types of brain scanning, particularly mapping of the brain using Magnetic Resonance Imaging (MRI). Proponents of the notion that dyslexia exists as a separate and distinctive form of reading difficulty claim that MRI scans demonstrate that there are differences in processing between the brains of dyslexic and non-dyslexic readers. This is where the circular argument comes in. In order to carry out these scans and to make statements about differences in brain structure and function, the scans are carried out on individuals already diagnosed as dyslexic by some other method. The research concerned with demonstrating that there is a population of pupils whose reading difficulties are different from the reading difficulties of other individuals is thus carried out on individuals who have already been defined as having this manifestly different problem in the first place.

Another reason to be cautious about making neurological links between reading failure and neurology is that of evidence. How do we know whether an intervention has produced neurological change? Not enough is known about the structure, functions and flexibility of our brains to be sure that we can effect lasting neurological change. This does not mean that we should not use specific interventions. If they work, continue to use them, irrespective of whether we can pinpoint any neurological change. If they don't work, try something else, because whether or not we are effecting neurological change, if the pupil is still failing to read then we have failed to teach. One of the dangers of assuming a specific cause for difficulties is that we fall into the trap of thinking that there is only one way to correct these difficulties. This can be seen in relation to dyslexia, where multi sensory teaching is an approach that is heavily promoted. Whilst this approach might well be successful in accelerating the progress of failing readers, it is by no means the only way. When we start to diagnose and attribute failure to factors such as neurology, there is a danger of adopting a prescription approach to remediation; that there is one and only one 'cure'.

You will probably have gathered that the issue of dyslexia is viewed with some scepticism by the authors! However, we are not trying to argue that the condition does not exist. There is certainly a group of pupils who do appear to experience specific difficulties with some or all aspects of literacy, but who do not appear to experience difficulties in other aspects of the curriculum. However, an explanation of these difficulties based *solely* on neurology (without a recognition of the impact of other factors such as the learning environment) can a pessimistic view of the capacity for improvement. We have both seen many children and young people diagnosed with dyslexia, who will quite openly (and sometimes cheerfully) state that there is nothing that can be done to help them because they have something wrong with their brain.

Summary

A biological view of learning emphasises the role of the brain in learning. All aspects of learning and memory have a neurological component. It is important to consider the range of convenience of the biological view. In terms of our role in schools, knowledge that the brain plays a vital role in learning is useful but in the absence of MRI scanners in school, we have to assume that changes might be occurring in children's brains as a result of their learning. We should also take care that a view of learning based solely on neurology does not lead us down the path of helplessness: the attitude that we can't effect change.

Professor Reuven Feurstein, whose work we look at in more detail later, takes a positive and optimistic view of our ability to learn. He says 'never let chromosomes have the last word' (meaning that we shouldn't make judgments about what we can or can't do on the basis of our genetic make up). Perhaps his saying could be extended to 'and neurones too'!

The biological dimension view of Jennifer

There are a number of factors in Jennifer's difficulties which relate to the biological dimension:

- the role of memory in learning (the information makes specific reference to memory problems)

- genetic predisposition (her mum has some learning difficulties)

- the role of the brain: perhaps Jennifer's difficulties are due to the fact that both hemispheres of her brain are not working in harmony

If you were working with Jennifer, how useful would these views be in helping you to deal with her difficulties more effectively? Rate their usefulness on a scale of 0 to 10, 0 being not at all useful and 10 being very useful. Make a note of your ratings, as we will ask you to compare them all after you have finished Part 3.

Reflection questions about the biological approach

In order to reflect on the content of this section, suggest some responses to the following questions about the use of teaching techniques that are based on neurology (such as the specific applications discussed in this section). If you have not used any of the techniques yourself, or observed them in use, try to talk with a colleague who has used them.

■ What evidence would suggest that the techniques are effective?

■ What evidence would suggest that the techniques are having an effect on pupils' brains?

What would be the long term outcomes of using these approaches, given that schools are mainly concerned with raising attainment? What would an individual using these techniques say about their impact on attainment?

The behavioural dimension

A behavioural theory of learning would basically define learning as a *change in observable behaviour.* These changes are brought about by a response to a stimulus and are repeated as a result of reinforcement of the observed behaviour (operant conditioning). In Part 3, we look at the way in which classical and operant theories are applied to learning.

One of the emphases in a behavioural approach is on observable behaviour. A biological view might argue that neurological changes take place (but we cannot see them), whereas a behaviourist would say that an *observable* change would be evidence that learning had occurred. An everyday example from the classroom might be as follows:

> Jenny could read aloud five sight words on Tuesday. On Friday she could read aloud ten sight words. We have observed a change in her reading behaviour (that is, an increase in the number of words she is able to read aloud), so we conclude that she has *learned* five new words.

Now let's take that example a step further and apply another central principle of behaviourism, that behaviour is strengthened by reinforcement. This reinforcement can be positive or negative.

> When Jenny read the sight words correctly, her classroom assistant nodded, smiled and said 'well done Jenny, you read all those words correctly'. Jenny was pleased when her classroom assistant spoke to her like that. When she was given the same words to read the next day she

again read them correctly. Unfortunately, Jenny's classroom assistant was away ill and another classroom assistant heard Jenny read. When Jenny had read her words, the new assistant said 'I'm not very impressed Jenny. You really should be able to read far more words than that at your age.' When Jenny was asked to read to this classroom assistant, she pretended to have a tummy ache so that she didn't have to read.

A behaviourist view of learning says that people can be trained to learn new skills by exposing them to a stimulus and then reinforcing the response to that stimulus. In the examples above, Jenny was exposed to a stimulus [the words to be read], she made a response [she read the words aloud correctly] and she received reinforcement [in the example, the positive reinforcement meant that Jenny repeated the behaviour of reading aloud and the negative reinforcement meant that Jenny avoided the behaviour of reading aloud].

B. F. Skinner, who is regarded as one of the leading theorists of *behaviourism*, developed something called 'programmed learning' as a result of his work about *operant* conditioning. He envisaged that programmed learning would be used by teaching machines (mechanical devices). However, the principles that he used for programming teaching machines were also used in relation to planning instruction that was not necessarily delivered mechanically. Programmed instruction consists of a sequenced method of planning and delivering instruction and includes careful attention to the steps involved in learning a skill (starting with a simple aspect and then moving to a more complex aspect) and the reinforcement given on completion of each step. Evaluation of learning outcomes is also a part of programmed learning, to ensure that steps and sequences are revised according to the response of the students.

Behavioural objectives

The emphasis on learning involving observable changes in behaviour led to a great deal of development in the way in which instruction is organised and presented. In 1962, Robert Mager published a highly influential work, *Preparing Instructional Objectives*. One of the means of ensuring that learning involved observable changes in behaviour was to make sure that the outcomes of learning were expressed in observable terms. The framework within which this instruction was designed and delivered was called a *criterion-referenced* framework. What this meant was that an evaluation of successful learning was judged against pre-set criteria, determined by the individual or institution making the assessment. This also meant that an individual could work through a programme of instruction at their own pace, provided that s/he met the criteria along the way. This type of assessment and evaluation is in contrast to *norm-referenced* assessment and evaluation, where judgments about an individual's performance are made by comparing performance to predetermined norms, usually related to expectations at a particular age. An important aspect of a criterion-referenced framework is to have clear objectives so that it is easy to state whether an individual has learned the requisite content. This is where behavioural objectives are used. A behavioural objective has three essential elements. These are:

Performance
This is a statement of what the pupil has to do. It should always contain an active verb; that is, a verb that describes an action that you can see.

Conditions
This is a description of the conditions under which the performance should take place. For example, a specification of how a task is presented to the pupil.

Criterion
This is a statement of the acceptable level of performance, such as how many words read correctly. The criterion sets the standard to be achieved for mastery of a task or skill.

Examples of behavioural objectives
Can name numbers one to five when numerals are presented randomly on flashcards, with no errors.

Can read aloud ten sight words when presented with words on flashcards, with no errors.

Can write the correct numeral underneath a drawing of a set of objects. Sets of objects presented randomly on a sheet of paper with sets no greater than 5 objects.

Useful verbs
Say, write, draw, read aloud, recite, draws, points to, underlines.

Verbs to avoid (because we cannot see or measure these actions)
Feel, think, appreciate, understand, like, discover, conclude, learn.

Task analysis
Task analysis is an extension of the use of behavioural objectives. As the title implies, it involves analysing a task. Sometimes, particularly in the case of pupils who are slow to learn, it is helpful to have the things we need to learn broken down into smaller steps. We learn one step and then go on to the next. If we do things in small steps, we can see the progress that we are making. For example, learning to read is an appropriate goal for all children. Just imagine, though, that you are starting school and are told that you will be successful when you have

Application activity: writing behavioural objectives

Choose a pupil with whom you are working.

Look at the literacy or numeracy skills you will be covering with this pupil during the coming week. This might be in the form of an IEP or part of focused planning by the class teacher for these areas.

Choose one aspect of this work and write a behavioural objective for it. If you have time, you could write several objectives for one part of your week's work.

Use the objective(s) to guide you when you teach the particular skill(s) to the pupil.

Was it easy to be able to say whether learning had taken place or not?

Why was this?

Are there areas of the curriculum where behavioural objectives are more or less useful?

What would be the advantages and disadvantages of writing an entire curriculum as behavioural objectives?

learned to read. This process might take a long time and you might well ask along the way 'how am I doing?' If the only goal is to learn to read, then you might be told very frequently that you had not succeeded because you had not met this learning goal. Typically, we break these big skills into much smaller steps. When we use task analysis, we take a skill and break it down into a series of smaller steps. These steps are written as behavioural objectives.

There is an example in the box below.

Task analysis for making a cup of tea

Fill the kettle with water

Plug in the kettle and turn on the electricity

Place a cup or mug next to the kettle

Place a teabag in the cup or mug

As soon as the water in the kettle has boiled, pour the boiling water into the cup. Fill almost to the top.

Leave for one minute

Using a spoon, squeeze the teabag against the side of the cup or mug

Throw away the teabag

If you drink tea with milk add the milk now. Or, if you drink tea with lemon, add a slice of lemon instead of the milk

If you like sugar in your tea, add it to the tea using a spoon

Stir the tea

Read through the example above, then answer these questions:

- Do the steps have to be done in that order?

- Which ones can or can't be changed?

- Can you think of a skill where it is very important for one step to be learned before the next?

- The task analysis has eleven steps. Does it always need to have 11 steps?

Application activity: writing a task analysis

Choose one attainment target from the National Curriculum, or a Stepping Stone from the Foundation Stage Curriculum.

Write a task analysis for the attainment target or Stepping Stone.

Shaping, forward chaining and backward chaining

Once we have written behavioural objectives and organised them into a task analysis of a skill, we can then think about using the techniques of shaping, forward chaining and backward chaining.

Shaping describes the way we reinforce successive approximations of the behaviour we are teaching. For example, if we were teaching a pupil to form letters, we might reinforce each close attempt to the letter form being written. At first we might not worry too much about a very precise copy, as long as it looks like the target letter or word. As we continue teaching, we would teach and reinforce closer matches to the target letter or word. However, we cannot always use shaping. In the task analysis example given above, it would not be desirable to observe behaviours close to the target behaviour (for example, it would be dangerous if we did not insist on filling the cup or mug *almost* to the top!)

Forward chaining is the term we use when we teach each step in the sequence from the beginning to the end. In the example above, we would start with step one and teach the steps in order up to step eleven. The pupil has to learn each step before he or she moves on to the next.

Backward chaining describes the situation when we teach the sequence in reverse. This is sometimes useful when we want the pupil to perform the desired skill. In the example above, we would carry out steps one to ten, then the pupil would do step eleven. When this step was learned, we would carry out steps one to nine and the pupil would do steps ten and eleven. Backward chaining is often used in life skills, such as dressing and undressing, so that the pupil achieves success in the skill quickly, but at the same time learns to do it for themselves.

An example might be teaching a child to put on socks. We would put the sock over the child's foot, pull it part way up the leg and then ask the child to pull it the rest of the way up the leg. Backward chaining also tells the pupil what the final behaviour is like.

The behavioural interactionist perspective of learning

The behavioural view of learning has so far concentrated on the B and C of the behavioural ABC that we met in the opening chapter. If you remember, the *behavioural* ABC is as follows:

A: Antecedents – the settings or contexts in which behaviour occurs.
B: Behaviour – observable behaviour.
C: Consequences – what happens after the behaviour occurs.

So far, the theories of learning derived from a behavioural view have focused on the way in which we can change consequences in order to encourage repetition of desired behaviour and that as a consequence of repetition, the behaviour is learned. We have focused on observable behaviour as a means of knowing whether learning has taken place.

One of the developments in behaviourism has been a growing emphasis on antecedents as well as consequences. This means that we can make changes to the settings or contexts in which behaviour occurs, as well as to the consequences, in order to produce changes in behaviour. The behavioural interactionist perspective proposed by Wheldall and Glynn shows how antecedents can also affect learning. They describe it as follows:

> ....in some respects, our perspective represents an attempt to implement child-centred learning within a behavioural framework ... It is behavioural, since it builds on the methods and principles of behavioural psychology. It is also interactionist, since it is based on the central idea that we all learn from each other by interacting with each other ... our concern is with using contemporary applied behaviour analysis to help teachers develop responsive social contexts for children so that effective learning can take place. (Wheldall and Glynn, 1989)

This perspective then shows us how our approach to learning can be broadened considerably from a purely operant conditioning viewpoint. An example of this broader view is seen in what Wheldall and Glynn call 'responsive social contexts'. These are described as settings in which control of learning is shared between a more and less skilled participant. Peer tutoring is an example of a responsive social context. Learning via peer tutoring means that a pupil is tutored by another pupil, sometimes of the same age or older. Research into peer tutoring shows that both tutor and the tutee improve their learning when this approach is used. Another way in which the behavioural interactionist perspective

Application activity: looking at antecedents

An antecedent is the context or setting in which behaviour occurs. This activity is designed to help you to consider the effect of antecedents on children's learning.

Choose a time when you can observe a class for about 30 to 45 minutes.

Sit somewhere where you can see what is going on, but also where you are as unobtrusive as possible.

The table below gives some examples of antecedents. There is also space for you to fill in your own examples. You might not observe all of the antecedents on the list. When you do observe the antecedent, note down next to it the effect you think it is having on the pupil's learning.

If you have time to reflect on your observations afterwards, you might want to think about whether the antecedents you have observed need to be changed, and if so, in what way.

Antecedent	Effect
Teacher instructions and explanations	
Layout of furniture	
Access to materials and resources needed for tasks	
Pupil initiation of learning interactions	
Teacher led discussion	

helps with learning is when we pay attention to the physical setting in which learning takes place. You may have experienced the negative effects of this if you have attended a course where the room was too hot/cold/large/small? If you have, after a time you were probably thinking more about how uncomfortable you felt, rather than what the course was about. The same applies to classrooms. Obviously, we can't always do anything about things like temperature or lighting, but we can pay attention to the layout of the room.

The layout of the classroom is an example of an antecedent, because it represents the context in which behaviour occurs. One well known study of the effect of antecedents in the classroom concerns rows and tables. Typically, primary classrooms are arranged in table groups. However, pupils do not always do group work. Often they are asked to do individual work, but are still seated in table groups. It is perhaps not surprising that pupils spend some of their time interacting with each other and not doing the set work. In the rows and tables research carried out by Wheldall *et al*, the on-task behaviour of a class of primary school pupils was observed under the usual classroom setting, that of table groups. Then the layout was changed to rows and further observations were carried out. Finally, the classroom was put back to its original and usual arrangement of table groups. Data from observations made during each phase of the study showed a very clear increase in on-task behaviour when the pupils were seated in rows. Furthermore, when the classroom was changed back from rows to tables, the pupils said that they preferred to be seated in rows!

Another antecedent that is likely to have a powerful effect on learning is the instruction given to pupils. Instructions and directions are an antecedent as they set the context for learning and usually precede behaviour. Try to count up how many instructions or directions you give to pupils during a typical school day. It will probably be quite a large number. So you are constantly affecting the antecedents for learning by how well you give instructions. If pupils are not clear about the tasks they have to undertake, the consequence is often off task or disruptive behaviour. Many of the instructions that we give are related to the delivery of the curriculum, so it is important that we give clear explanations and instructions, otherwise learning might not take place. This point is covered in more detail in the next section, where the instructional dimension of learning is considered.

Summary

Much of the information in this section comes from research carried out during the middle of the twentieth century. Even the more recent behavioural interactionist perspective was proposed almost twenty years ago. However, it is interesting to reflect on the way in which these ideas still have an influence on education in the twenty-first century. For example, more than half a century after Skinner was carrying out his work, we are being urged to write SMART targets for Individual Education Plans (IEPs). SMART targets are **s**pecific, **m**easurable, **a**chievable, **r**ealistic and **t**ime related. Skinner's influence can certainly be seen in the specific, measurable and time related criteria. If these criteria are met, then we are likely to see learning in terms of observable changes in behaviour, which is the behaviourist definition of learning. Techniques such as shaping, backward chaining and forward chaining are still used in work with pupils deemed to have severe and/or complex learning difficulties. However, we do also need to consider whether the use of a behavioural definition of learning could narrow the focus of what is taught. Do we always have to be able to see or measure something in order to say that learning has taken place? Perhaps we can do this when we are talking about specific skills, but it is harder when we begin to think about our motivation to learn, or interest in learning, a specific skill. A behaviourist might argue that even these aspects of behaviour would still come down to something observable; for example, we might say that a pupil is more interested in reading if we observed him reading more books.

It is the range of convenience that should be considered when we think about the usefulness of the various theories about learning. There is no doubt that behaviourism has made a useful and lasting contribution to the way in which we organise instruction and evaluate its impact, especially in relation to skills that lend themselves to being expressed in observable terms. If we want to find out whether learning has taken place, an emphasis on the observable will generally leave little room for doubt. However, although we can't observe or measure everything involved in learning, neither should we leave our evaluation of learning to pure speculation.

The behavioural dimension view of Jennifer
There are a number of factors in Jennifer's difficulties that would be identified by the behavioural dimension. These are:

- use of behavioural objectives in order to give clear and unambiguous targets for her learning

- task analysis of the next steps of learning. Some of the NLS targets and National Curriculum attainment targets might need to be broken down into smaller steps

- we must see an observable change in order to know that Jennifer has learned

If you were the teaching assistant working with Jennifer, how useful are the above emphases in helping you to intervene in Jennifer's difficulties more effectively? Rate their usefulness on a scale of nought to ten, nought being not useful at all and ten being very useful. Make a note of your ratings, as we will ask you to compare them all after you have finished Part 3.

The instructional dimension
Theories of learning in the *instructional dimension* define learning in relation to instruction and view teaching and learning as a continuous and inseparable process. Learning, in this dimension, can be said to have occurred as a result of instruction. The reverse view would also apply, that if learning has not occurred, then neither has teaching. Therefore, learning is dependent on the quality and appropriateness of instruction. In the introduction to this section, we defined learning as involving change. In the instructional dimension, this change is brought about by the interaction of the learner with the teaching environment. Therefore, in this dimension, a definition of learning would be changes brought about by instruction. Theories of learning based on an instructional model emphasise the following:

■ The organisation of instruction
■ The design of instruction
■ The delivery of instruction

The learning hierarchy

The learning hierarchy was proposed by Haring, Lovitt, Eaton and Hansen in 1978. It has been included in the instructional dimension, since each stage of the hierarchy can be seen as being dependent on adequate and appropriate instruction.

The stages of the hierarchy are shown in the table below. An example of a skill that many adults learn is included in the table: learning to drive.

Stage of hierarchy	Explanation	Example
Acquisition	The skill to be learned is 'brand new' to the learner. The learner has to be able to perform the skill accurately and at this stage probably has to put a lot of conscious effort into demonstrating the skill.	Our first driving lessons! We learn what the controls are for and where they are. We learn the basics of use of the accelerator, clutch and brakes. We begin to co-ordinate all these aspects of driving in order to make the car move! We probably have to think carefully about what to do at each stage of driving: for example, when to depress the clutch and change gear.
Fluency	Once the skill is performed accurately, the learner goes through a period of repeated practise so that s/he is able to perform the skill fluently as well as accurately. This means that the skill can be performed with a minimum of effort; it is almost automatic.	We are able to coordinate all the necessary actions in order to drive the car. We have lots more lessons so that we can perform the sequence of actions fluently, without really thinking. Actions such as 'mirror, signal, manouevre' become automatic.
Maintenance	This is the point at which the skill will be maintained, since a fluent and accurate performance means that the learner is less likely to forget the skill. We call this mastery.	We are able to drive fluently and accurately and will probably have mastered the skill sufficiently well in order to pass our driving test.
Generalisation	With instruction, the learner uses the skill in different settings or with different materials.	After we have passed the driving test, we take additional lessons in order to do motorway driving, or to be an advanced driver.
Adaptation	Without instruction, the learner uses the skill in different settings or with different materials.	We drive in another country. We drive different vehicles.

The *learning hierarchy* is useful because it helps us to plan the way in which we teach a skill to a pupil in order to make sure that the skill is retained. The time that an individual pupil will take to achieve each stage of the hierarchy will vary. There are no rules about how long it will take to acquire a skill. This is an important consideration when we think about teaching pupils with special educational needs. Use of the hierarchy to guide teaching means that we move through each stage at the pupil's pace. Success is then more likely since we will have spent an appropriate amount of time developing both fluency and accuracy.

The learning hierarchy also gives us another perspective on the notion of special educational needs, especially in relation to pupils who rarely seem to retain any skills. An instructional approach, based on the learning hierarchy, would define learning difficulties in relation to accuracy and fluency in skill performance. A pupil who forgets skills is seen as a pupil who has not yet mastered the skill due to insufficient time spent on the acquisition and fluency stages. This is an optimistic view of learning difficulties. By attributing the difficulties to the quality and quantity of instruction, we are saying that we can influence this process and as a result produce more effective learning. Contrast this to a view of learning difficulties that simply views the child as being unable to learn. Often the reasons being given are related to assumed neurological problems or theories about overall intelligence.

Reflection point: applying the hierarchy to our learning

Think of a skill that you learned to do fairly easily. How much time did you spend practising this skill?

Now think of a skill that you found very difficult to learn. How much time did you spend practising this skill?

Were the amounts of time the same?

If you had set a time limit on learning the more difficult skill, do you think you would have learned it properly? Think about the reason for your response.

Now think about a pupil that you work with, who has difficulties in learning. What do you do to help the pupil to become fluent in a skill? Does the pupil find it difficult when there are time limits imposed on the time available to practise a skill?

What are the implications for the way in which we teach pupils with learning difficulties?

If we accept that accuracy and fluency are important aspects of learning and retaining skills, then it is useful to have a means of knowing when appropriate levels of accuracy and fluency have been achieved. If we know this, we can make an informed decision about when to move on to the next skill(s), whilst feeling confident that the pupil won't forget what s/he has just learned. The next part of this section deals with Precision Teaching, which is a means of establishing whether a pupil has learned a skill with sufficient accuracy and fluency for us to be able to say that the skill has been mastered.

Precision Teaching

One of the first things to say about Precision Teaching is that it has a very misleading title. Precision Teaching is not a method of teaching. It is a method of evaluating teaching in order to find out what works for individual pupils. This monitoring is done by sampling both accuracy and fluency in the performance of skills, in order to determine whether a skill has been mastered, and therefore is likely to be retained.

Precision Teaching was developed during the 1950s and 1960s by Ogden Lindsley. Lindsley was a behavioural psychologist, who was a student of B. F. Skinner. Lindsley applied the idea of free operant conditioning to classroom learning. Free operant conditioning is operating when pupils can respond to instruction at their own pace and where the instruction or materials do not place restrictions on learning. This meant that when applied to school learning, the fluency of a pupil's response is as important as accuracy. This point is illustrated by the following example:

> You are marking some maths exercises carried out by your pupils, that involve giving the answers to addition sums, where the totals go up to twenty. You are really pleased because they all scored ten out of ten. You conclude that your group of pupils have learned addition to twenty. But ... then you realise that two of the pupils in the group spent an hour doing this page of sums, whereas the rest of the group did them in five minutes.

> Have all the pupils learned addition to twenty?

> If your answer is no, why not?

Pupils who took an hour to complete the exercise to have not learned the skill thoroughly. If we only look at accuracy scores, we can never be really certain that a pupil has learned a skill.

Precision Teaching is a means of monitoring both accuracy and fluency, so we can decide when a pupil has mastered a skill and consequently when it is appropriate to move on to the next skill we want to teach. Although Precision Teaching is included in the instructional dimension of learning, it could also be included in the behavioural dimension, since it has its roots in a behaviourist view. The behaviourist dimension is reflected in the demand that Precision Teaching focuses on observable behaviours, because we are evaluating teaching by measuring the pupil's skill performance. Precision Teaching involves taking a timed sample of skill performance, then making a judgment about skill mastery based on pre-determined criteria related to accuracy and fluency; *how many* and *how quickly.*

A number of steps are involved in implementing Precision Teaching. The table below outlines these steps, with an example.

Precision Teaching step	Example
Determine the skill to be taught and express it as an observable behaviour. Use a *behavioural* objective format in order to do this (see the paragraph entitled *behavioural objectives* in the previous section of this chapter: The Behavioural Dimension).	Jessica will read sight words aloud from a probe sheet.* * a probe sheet is a specially prepared sheet that is used when sampling accuracy and fluency in Precision Teaching. An example will be given below.
Determine the level of performance for both accuracy and fluency	The sight words will be read at the rate of 50 correct in one minute, with no more than two mistakes.
Take a sample of the specified behaviour on a daily basis	Every day, Jessica will be given a probe sheet with the sight words written down in a random order. She will be asked to read the words out loud and will be timed for 1 minute exactly
Record the data on a chart	See example below
Look at the data and decide whether you need to change Jessica's programme	Once you have recorded data on a chart for a maximum of eight days, you can see how close Jessica is to reaching the target set in step two. If she is nowhere near this target, then her task should be changed. Perhaps you are introducing too many new words at once. Try 'slicing' the task (that is, breaking it into smaller pieces. For example, if ten new words are introduced at a time, a task slice would be to introduce five new words at a time).

Precision Teaching looks at improvements in performance, by recording data on a special chart called a celeration or semi-logarithmic chart. This is a special type of graph that tells us how much a performance has accelerated (rather than just increased). For example, if Jessica reads one word correctly on Monday and two words correctly on Tuesday, she has doubled her performance. The improvement, or acceleration, from one to two is greater than an increase from, say, 90 to 100, even though 90 to 100 is an increase of ten words. Hopefully the example of a completed chart below will illustrate the point about how improvement in performance is measured and judged.

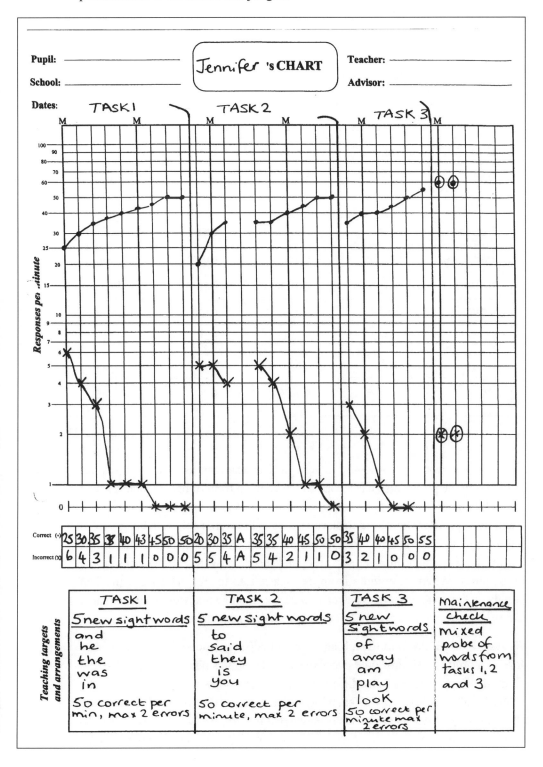

Skills are often sampled on a *probe chart*. This is a prepared sheet containing examples of the skill in a random presentation. An example is shown below.

Jessica's probe sheet

Skill to be increased: Sight words

Performance: 50 correct per minute, maximum two errors

dog	ball	house	baby	mum
ball	dog	baby	mum	house
baby	ball	dog	house	mum
house	baby	mum	dog	ball
ball	house	dog	mum	baby
mum	baby	house	ball	dog
house	dog	ball	mum	baby
dog	baby	house	ball	mum
mum	ball	dog	baby	house
ball	house	baby	dog	mum

This sheet of words is presented to Jessica. Her teaching assistant, who is administering the probe, also has a copy of the sheet in front of her. Jessica is asked to read as many words as she can in one minute. She is told when to start and when to stop. After she is told to start, she reads the words across the page, from left to right, and she is timed for one minute exactly. As Jessica reads the words, her teaching assistant marks the correct and incorrect words on her copy of the probe sheet. When the minute is up, Jessica is told to stop. Her assistant then counts up how many words were read correctly and how many errors were made. These data are then transferred onto Jessica's Precision Teaching chart.

As stated earlier, Precision Teaching is not actually a method of teaching. Therefore, if a probe is administered every day and the pupil's performance noted and charted, it is unlikely that any differences would be seen, since administering the probe is not a substitute for teaching the skill. Therefore, Precision Teaching should be used after teaching has been carried out. Typically, a Precision Teaching programme consists of a period of teaching, followed by administration of the probe and charting of data. The charted data are then scrutinised in order to decide what to do next. The next steps can be one of several options:

■ continue with the current programme as the pupil is close to the level of performance stipulated for mastery

■ slice the task as progress towards mastery is too slow

■ change the task altogether, because the pupil might not have mastered some of the pre-requisite skills

■ use strategies to motivate the pupil

■ change the teaching approach

The changes would be introduced one at a time. Teaching, probing and charting would then be continued and the data on the chart examined again after a period of time, a minimum of three days and maximum of eight days. Any changes in the data can then be linked to the change in task or teaching arrangements that have been made. Precision Teaching therefore helps to tell us what size of task and which teaching approach work best for the pupil.

Application exercise: administering a probe

Choose one of your pupils, preferably one who requires extra help with some aspect of reading. Look at the current programme for this pupil and make a list of ten words that s/he is learning to read by sight. Make a probe sheet of these words (see the example shown earlier).

Administer the probe for one minute exactly. Note down the number that are correct and incorrect over a minute.

What do these results tell you about this pupil's accuracy and fluency in performing this skill?

If you have not looked at fluency and accuracy before, think about how this might influence your teaching in the future.

There are many advantages for teachers and teaching assistants in using Precision Teaching, such as:

■ it does not require a great deal of time every day but it does give clear and quick feedback about the pupil's learning

■ it can tell us whether the pupil's rate of learning is appropriate: whether the pupil is learning fast enough

■ it can tell us whether the pupil is mastering the skills we are teaching

■ it is an efficient way of keeping records of pupil progress. One chart gives six weeks of data

■ pupils usually find the approach very motivating, especially if they are able to chart their own data

■ it gives a clear message to pupils about the expectations for learning, so there can be no disagreement about whether targets have been met or not. This can be particularly useful for pupils who have low self-esteem in relation to learning. You have probably come across pupils who never seem to believe you when you tell them their work is improving. With Precision Teaching, the goals you set are observable and measurable. Therefore you can use the data as a means of recognising and celebrating improvements

It is worth trying out this method of monitoring, especially as teaching assistants often have more time to devote to seeing pupils individually on a daily basis. This approach will take up a maximum of ten minutes per pupil, which includes a period of teaching before the probe is administered and the data charted. It is outside the scope of this book to give detailed instructions about how to set up and implement a Precision Teaching Programme. Your school SENCo or Educational Psychologist should be able to help you to set one up.

Direct Instruction

Direct Instruction (DI) was developed by Siegfried Englemann and Carl Bereiter in the 1960s. It falls into the *instructional* dimension of learning, as the goal of DI is to accelerate learning through efficient instruction. This is achieved by careful attention to the organisation and delivery of instruction. DI is often referred to as 'drills and skills' by those who do not fully understand the methodology, since it can appear to be a very mechanical way of teaching. However, the reality is far removed from this narrow view of drills and skills, since Englemann developed DI as a result of thinking about issues of generalisation and transfer of learning. Direct instruction involves analysis of the knowledge required, of the communication between teacher and pupils and of pupil behaviour. When these are analysed, it is possible to design effective instruction. Therefore, a DI approach analyses the domain of knowledge such as reading, maths, science etc into logical and related sequences for teaching. Then attention is given to exactly how the teacher will communicate these teaching steps to the pupils, with an emphasis on clear and precise communication. Finally, pupil behaviour is analysed in order to ensure that the responses required of pupils indicate whether content and/or skills have been mastered. An important feature of the way in which instruction is organised in DI is an emphasis on generalisation. This is done by teaching strategies, rather than isolated skills. The box below gives an example of the way in which strategies are taught in a phonics teaching programme.

Scope and sequence: phonics teaching in a typical DI package

The first initial letter sounds taught are, for example:

m, n, f, s, a

It is possible to 'hold the sound' of these letters; that is, we can say the sound and keep saying it (like saying 'mmmmmm' when you've had something nice to eat!)

These types of sounds are taught first because if we can hold sounds we can also learn the **strategy** of blending sounds together.

Therefore, in a typical DI programme, the five sounds listed above are taught and immediately afterwards pupils are taught to blend. For example:

Two letter blends: an, fa, sa, na

Which then lead on to

Three letter blends: man, fan, nan

Therefore, the pupil learns five letter sounds and very quickly after that is beginning to read three letter consonant-vowel-consonant (CVC) words. Subsequent introduction of more letter sounds uses the same blending strategy, so that the skill is generalised to reading a range of phonically regular words. In contrast, many phonic programmes teach all 26 letter sounds before introducing blending. In this type of teaching sequence, it is a considerable time before the pupil is taught a strategy for using the letter sounds that s/he has learned.

In Direct Instruction, the sequence of instruction is arranged so that there is a logical order to teaching, with teaching steps organised according to complexity and utility. High utility skills are taught first, and exceptions are taught later; easy skills or concepts are taught before more difficult ones and component skills are taught in a logical and sequenced order. When a skill has been taught, transfer is always addressed. This means that the instruction guides the pupil into generalising and applying the skill. Here we can see the influence of the learning hierarchy. One of the ways in which instruction is made efficient in a DI approach is via the use of scripts and formats. The DI approach aims to minimise any confusion that might arise as a result of unclear instructions. In addition, DI believes that time is potentially wasted if a teacher spends every lesson re explaining tasks. Therefore, scripts and formats are used in order to minimise time spent in explaining. A *script* is just what the word implies. A DI teaching programme will include a script for the teacher so that instructions and explanations are delivered with maximum clarity. A *format* is a particular sequence of instruction. Its purpose is to ensure that familiarity with the instructional procedure means that a minimum amount of time is spent in explaining teaching procedures and the way in which pupils should respond. The table below gives an example of a teaching format typically found in DI, called *model, lead, test, review*.

Step	What it means	Example	Script used with pupils	Form of words used with pupils when they are accustomed to the format
Model	The teacher demonstrates the skill to the pupils	The teacher reads new sight words aloud to the pupils	'Listen whilst I read these words. It's my turn to read'	'My turn'
Lead	The pupils imitate the teacher	The pupils repeat the words after the teacher	'When I say the word, you say it after me. You are going to be my echo'	'Be my echo'
Test	Pupils perform the skill without assistance	The pupils read the words on their own	'Now you're going to read each word on your own. Read the word aloud when I point to it and say what word'	'What word?'
Review	As for test, but after a period of time has elapsed	As for test	As for test	As for test

The last column in the table shows the 'shorthand' that can be developed in order to minimise the time spent in explaining teaching procedures. Clearly, time has to be spent when the procedures are being introduced to pupils; when they are instructionally naïve. After a short time it is possible to use the shortened form of words for each step of the format as there will be shared understanding of what each term means.

As the design methodology involved in Direct Instruction can be extremely complex and time consuming to develop, this approach is most commonly found in commercial packages, which means that teachers can deliver a DI programme and learn about the methodology as they go along, rather than learning the methodology first and then using it with pupils. The packaging of DI approaches into ready made programmes highlights another distinctive feature of DI, which is field testing. In order to ensure that ready prepared programmes are successful, extensive field testing is carried out prior to making any programme available widely. These packages utilise scripts and formats and are usually delivered to groups of pupils, which highlights another feature of the DI methodology, that of unison responding. This is when pupils respond as a group, rather than individually. For example, if the task involves reading words or letter sounds, the pupils would read these together.

The effectiveness of Direct Instruction methodology is backed up by a substantial body of research. One of the largest research projects carried out in the United States was called *Project Follow Through*. This research was a large-scale evaluation of a number of teaching methods and approaches. 75,000 children were followed up between 1967 and 1995 in order to evaluate the impact of twelve different approaches to teaching, one of which was DI. The research found that DI had the most impact on attainments in basic skills, cognitive skills and self esteem. Examples of other approaches evaluated were *High/Scope* (a particular approach to the Nursery/Early Years Curriculum), language-based approaches and developmental approaches.

Follow up activity

Just as we said with Precision Teaching, it isn't possible for this book to provide all the necessary training in order to implement the different methodologies we have covered. This also applies to the use of Direct Instruction. However, as a follow-up, you might want to find out whether any packages are used in your school, talk with staff who are using them and possibly observe some lessons. The type of commercial packages available are:

- *Corrective Reading* (for Secondary aged pupils, published by SRA/McGraw Hill)

- *Beginning Reading* or *Basic Reading* (individual reading packages published by OTSU)

- *Companion Reading* (a group reading package for Primary aged children, published by OTSU)

If DI is not being used, you could talk to your school SENCo or Educational Psychologist if you are interested in using this methodology yourself.

Advance organisers

Advance organisers is a term suggested by the psychologist David Ausubel. His work is included in the instructional dimension, since the notion of advance organisers is an instructional device designed to assist learning. An advance organiser is something that helps the learner to make connections between new and previous learning. Ausubel thought of knowledge (and therefore learning) as hierarchical. When we learn, we organise material hierarchically by placing knowledge into categories, some of which are superordinate categories. This concept was discussed in the section on memory: look back at the biological dimension section where the discussion of memory examines the role of categorisation. An advance organiser helps the learner to fit new knowledge into existing categories. Ausubel identifies two types of advance organiser. *Expository organisers* give new knowledge in order to help the learner understand the lesson. For example, in a maths lesson, the teacher might introduce the concept of length by defining it for the pupils and linking it to the superordinate concept of measurement. *Comparative organisers* give new knowledge by making comparisons or drawing analogies with familiar knowledge. For example, a lesson about grids in maths might be related to children playing the game of battleships. Ausubel's idea of advance organisers leads to a set of principles for instruction; firstly, that general ideas are presented first and are then followed by more detailed and specific information; secondly, that any new learning should be linked to any prior information. He calls the process of learning *subsumption*, where new knowledge is related to relevant prior knowledge, within the learner's existing cognitive structures.

Summary

In this section, we have considered the role of instruction in learning. The basic premise is that if learning has not taken place, then neither has teaching. The wealth of guidance now given to schools and teachers, both statutory and non-statutory, is mainly related to what is taught, that is, to curriculum content rather than how instruction should be delivered – even though the quality of instruction is the one factor that will make a difference to learning. The implementation of the literacy and numeracy hours in school began to look at the role of instruction. For example in the numeracy hour, there are elements of direct instruction methodology in the whole class interactive teaching part of the strategy. One of the reasons for the shift in focus from content to methodology was that studies of countries where literacy and numeracy attainments were higher than the UK suggested that it was the teaching method, rather than the content, which made a difference to pupil attainment.

Psychology can tell us how people learn. If we understand the process of learning then we can think about what to do if things go wrong. The focus of this section on instruction provides some very useful starting points for thinking about why a pupil is not learning, and what can be done about it. A common response by schools to a pupil's failure to learn is to change the materials being used. Think about this in relation to your situation. Have you worked with a pupil who has reading difficulties? What is the most frequent strategy used? We suggest that what often happens is the pupil is given a different scheme or set of

---

Example and application activity: using advance organisers

Here is an example of an *advance organiser*, taken from the content of this book. In this section we have met new information about *Precision Teaching* (PT). A definition was given of this technique and it was linked to superordinate knowledge by making reference to its use of *behavioural* objectives and the fact that it can be placed in the behavioural dimension as well as the instructional. An analogy that can be drawn for PT is that it is a bit like the 'plan, do, review' cycle that is found in *High/Scope,* since we use PT to plan what we are going to do and then to evaluate its effectiveness. Another analogy (for those unfamiliar with *High/Scope*) is that it can be compared with the process of criterion referenced assessment, where we carry out an intervention and evaluate its impact according to criteria determined at the outset (in the case of PT, these criteria relate to the accuracy and fluency measures).

Another example of an *advance organiser* is the comparison made with learning to drive when we looked at the learning hierarchy.

Try doing some advance organisers yourself. Choose a topic, or aspect of a subject, that you know you will be working on with your pupils. You might need to ask the class or subject teacher for a copy of his or her short-term planning so that you know what new material will be covered with the class.

Choose just one new piece of information that is going to feature in the lesson.

Write down the *advance organisers* for this new information. This should include:

- ▪ How the new knowledge is linked to superordinate concepts

- ▪ How the new knowledge can be compared with existing knowledge

If you are responsible for delivering any part of this new information, try using the advance organisers you have prepared. Afterwards, reflect on the usefulness of this technique.

books to work through. Sometimes this change is from the usual reading scheme used in school to a 'rescue' scheme designed for failing readers such as *Fuzz-buzz* or *Wellington Square*. Often the pupil continues to fail to learn to read and typically, two things happen. Either the pupil becomes stuck on a particular level of the scheme ('s/he's been reading the same book for the last term'), or goes through every scheme available in school and still can't read ('we haven't got anything else in school s/he can read'). These scenarios are missing the point about the pupil's failure. The instruction given is the one thing that is unlikely to have changed. If we have an understanding of the role of instruction in learning, we can look beyond any supposed deficiencies in the pupil and begin to look at the impact of instruction on learning. Then we can make changes which will benefit the pupil.

The instructional dimension view of Jennifer

There are a number of factors in Jennifer's difficulties that are relevant to the *instructional* dimension. These are as follows:

- if Jennifer isn't learning, the instruction isn't appropriate and should therefore be changed
- forgetting might be due to poor skill mastery. Jennifer has not developed sufficient accuracy and fluency in basic skills, such as word recognition and phonics
- some difficulties might be due to lack of development of pre-requisite skills
- she might cope better with her reading book if she had some advance organisers

If you were the teaching assistant working with Jennifer, how useful are the above points in helping you to intervene more effectively in Jennifer's difficulties? Rate their usefulness on a scale of nought to ten, nought being not at all useful and ten being very useful. Make a note of your ratings, as we will ask you to compare them all after you have finished Part 3.

The social constructivist dimension

This dimension emphasises the role of social factors in the process of learning. Therefore, the change aspect of learning is attributed, at least in part, to the effect of social factors. Learning, in this view, is related to social factors, such as transmission of culture or interactions between individuals and their environments. In the social constructivist dimension, learning is viewed as something that is an active, interactive process which involves meaning and understanding. In this section, we will examine the work of three psychologists: Vygotsky, Feurstein and Bruner.

The work of Lev Vygotsky

Vygotsky was a Russian psychologist. His work was not well known in the West until recently, due to the separation of much of Communist Eastern Europe from the rest of the world. Vygotsky emphasised the role of social interaction in the intellectual development of the child. He proposed three stages of intellectual development: a first stage where action and trial and error behaviour are most apparent, a second stage where the child begins to use strategies, and a third stage where the child is able to integrate several strategies. One of the best known theories of Vygotsky is the *zone of proximal development* (ZPD). The ZPD is the distance between the actual level of development and the potential level of development. This 'potential level' is demonstrated when the child has access to mediation or guidance from a more skilled individual. The ZPD encapsulates the social construction of learning emphasised by Vygotsky, since the child demonstrates a higher level of achievement in a collective or collaborative activity. The idea of *scaffolding* was proposed by Vygotsky as part of the ZPD theory. *Scaffolding* takes place in the ZPD and is a process whereby the process of collaborative learning gradually shifts from the more experienced learner doing most of the task to the learner doing most or all of the task. Scaffolding keeps learners in the ZPD. Vygotsky proposed that play was a means of observing the ZPD, since children often performed above their actual developmental levels when engaged in play. He described the child in a play situation as being 'a head taller than himself'.

The work of Reuven Feurstein

Reuven Feurstein's work draws on and expands the theories of Piaget and Vygotsky. Feurstein was a pupil of Piaget. Just after the Second World War his job as a psychologist involved administering intelligence tests to adolescent immigrants (including Holocaust survivors) arriving in the newly created state of Israel, in order to place these young people in appropriate educational settings. The results of the tests showed that a very high proportion of these young people had low intelligence – many more than would be expected – and he began to question whether the tests were a true reflection of the young people's capabilities. The one thing that all these individuals had in common was that they had been traumatised by their experiences of the Holocaust, or of being separated from their culture due to the effects of war. Feurstein's experience led him to develop the theory of *structural cognitive modifiability*. There are several key concepts in this theory:

■ he recognises two types of learning: direct learning and mediated learning. Direct learning is a concept from Piaget, and involves direct interaction between the learner and stimuli from the environment. Mediated learning involves the presence of a mediator between the learner and the stimuli. The mediator selects and organises stimuli appropriate for the learner. Through this process the cognitive structure of the child is affected. Direct learning is usually adequate for most learners, since they can assimilate new stimuli with prior learning ('assimilation' is a term used by Piaget). However, for some learners, there are factors that interfere with their ability to profit from direct learning, so although learning does occur, it may occur haphazardly. In this situation, the learner needs mediation

■ learning cannot be separated from experience and culture

■ intelligence is not fixed. It is defined by Feurstein as the process by which humans are modified. He describes intelligence as *cognitive flexibility and adaptability*. The consequence of flexibility and adaptability is that individuals can change and develop their ability to think.

Feurstein proposes that intellectual development is affected by access to mediated learning experience (MLE). The amount of access to MLE explains why some learners show deficiencies in their thinking. Feurstein believes that all humans can be modified, in spite of factors of age, the cause of the difficulty and the severity of the difficulty. He calls these three factors 'challenges' to learning rather than barriers. He accepts elements of cognitive functioning outlined by Piaget, but rejects the notion that the development of thinking can be packaged into developmental stages or that there are critical periods for intellectual development. Feurstein uses the term *tripartite learning partnership* to describe learning. The three elements of this partnership are:

■ the learner – Feurstein suggests a list of *cognitive functions* that are observed in the learner. We might be more familiar with the terms *thinking skills* or *process skills*. Cognitive functions are skills such as planning, exploring stimuli systematically, comparing, categorising or labelling

■ the mediator – who mediates stimuli and experiences to the learner

■ the task itself – Feurstein proposes a way of analysing tasks by looking, for example, at how complex or abstract a task is

The process of learning is an interaction between these three elements of the partnership.

Practical applications of Feurstein's theories are found in a means of assessment called Dynamic Assessment and in teaching programmes such as Instrumental Enrichment and Bright Start. Dynamic Assessment is a way of assessing the cognitive functions of the learner in an interactive context where the assessor is able to intervene during assessment in order to identify the next steps of learning. Instrumental Enrichment is a cognitive education programme for pupils aged 10 and upwards and Bright Start is a cognitive education programme for early years pupils, developed by Professor Carl Hayward.

Having read about thinking skills, take a moment to reflect on their use in the classroom. First of all, think about the sorts of activities you do with your pupils. This is probably planned by class or subjects teachers, using the national curriculum, national literacy strategy and national numeracy strategy to plan work for the pupils. When you think about your work with pupils, the chances are that most of it is related to content, that is *what* the pupils need to learn. You are probably not given much guidance about *how* pupils should learn. Thinking skills help us to be clear about how learning takes place. The development of thinking skills helps pupils to become effective and independent learners.

Although you may decide that much of the work you do with pupils is content driven, the National Curriculum does take account of the importance of thinking skills. In 1998, a project was initiated by the Department for Education and Employment to look at the role of thinking skills in classrooms. This work was carried out by Carol McGuinness. The National Curriculum online contains information and resources related to thinking skills.

Follow up activity: finding out about thinking skills

Look at the National Curriculum on line at www.nc.uk.net

Select 'Learning Across the Curriculum'

In this section, you will find information about thinking skills. You can choose a Key Stage and a subject area, then search for teaching ideas related to a number of thinking skills.

When you have browsed at these pages, do some specific planning related to the work you are doing with your pupils. Ask one of the teachers you work with for a copy of his or her weekly plan that includes the work you are going to do with either individual or groups of pupils.

Look at the plan in relation to the thinking skills on the National Curriculum website. Could you identify at least one thinking skill that would help the pupil(s) to complete the set work? Can you also think of other subjects or activities where exactly the same thinking skill would be useful?

The work of Jerome Bruner

Jerome Bruner was a *developmental* psychologist. His work could have been included in the developmental section, as he proposed a model for intellectual development, or in the instructional section, as his theories make specific reference to the role of instruction in learning. We have placed Bruner alongside Vygotsky and Feurstein due to the *constructivist* emphasis of his theories. Whilst Vygotsky and Feurstein emphasise the *social constructivist* elements of learning (that is, learning is an interactive process), Bruner emphasises the *constructivist* element of learning, that is, that learning occurs when the learner organises new knowledge and experiences using previous and present knowledge. The learner therefore actively *constructs* learning. This process can be compared with Piaget's ideas of assimilation and accommodation which are described in the developmental section.

One of Bruner's proposals was that of *discovery learning*. This occurs when pupils find things out for themselves, but the teacher arranges activities and experiences to achieve this and makes sure that any preparation required is made. Discovery learning is not, therefore, an unstructured free for all, but a carefully planned learning experience. It is unfortunate that discovery learning has been represented as a process that regards teacher intervention as highly undesirable because it prevents children from finding out for themselves. This has led to the worst of practice in the nursery and infant classes in which the staff feel it is enough simply to offer a range of activities and experiences to children. Discovery learning is structured and planned, not something that happens by accident.

Bruner's view of learning fits in with those of Vygotsky and Feurstein in that he sees learning as an active process. However, his view of discovery learning departs from theirs, since it does not emphasise an active role for the more experienced learner, for example, as a mediator or as the provider of scaffolding in the ZPD. In Bruner's view, the adult or teacher is a facilitator and not always the active, collaborative participant of Feurstein and Vygotsky.

Summary

For the psychologists whose work we have considered in this section, learning is far more than mere absorption of facts or training in the acquisition of skills. In the *social constructivist* dimension, learning has a social, interactive component which transmits the culture and values of the group in a dynamic way.

This dimension has much to offer schools in terms of the cultural diversity that is now an aspect of 21st century society. If learning is a social activity that involves an element of cultural transmission, failure to learn will mean that this does not take place. In the *social constructivist* dimension, we must be careful not to learn using criteria that are socially or culturally inappropriate to judge failure. Questions we should be asking are: 'who decides what constitutes learning?'; 'by whose standards are we judging failure to learn?' If the curriculum has a strong white Eurocentric bias, it is surprising that pupils who are not white or of European background find it difficult to access that curriculum?

Many of the above issues form part of the debate about what we mean by intelligence and IQ and how we measure these.

The social constructivist dimension view of Jennifer

There are a number of factors in Jennifer's difficulties that the *social constructivist* dimension would identify. These are as follows:

- Jennifer's difficulties are due to a lack of mediation. We need to learn how to mediate to her

- Jennifer has not yet developed the thinking skills necessary to succeed with subjects such as reading and maths

If you were the teaching assistant working with Jennifer, how useful are the above points in helping you to intervene in Jennifer's difficulties more effectively? Rate their usefulness on a scale of nought to ten, nought being not at all useful and ten being very useful. Make a note of your ratings, as we will ask you to compare them all after you have finished Part 3.

The experiential dimension

The *experiential* dimension views learning as relating to personal change, which means that the change element of learning we have identified as the root of our definition, is a personal experience in this dimension and takes place as a result of the individual reflecting on experience.

The work of Carl Rogers

Carl Rogers is known best for his theories relating to counselling and therapy. His work comes under the *humanistic* aspect of psychology considered in the introduction to theories at the beginning of this book, but he related his theories to education and learning. Rogers' approach to counselling and therapy is a *person-centered* approach. This means that in a relationship between client and therapist, the client usually knows what they want and the therapist's task is to be a facilitator to help the client achieve their goals. To be a facilitator, the therapist has to take a non-directive stance within the client/therapist relationship; he helps to clarify the client's thoughts, but does not direct them. This means that interpersonal relationships are an important aspect of this type of approach so as to create a non-threatening atmosphere within which the therapy takes place, and to enable the client to develop a relationship of trust with the therapist.

Rogers applied these ideas to education in his book *Freedom to Learn* (1969). In a Rogerian view of learning, the teacher is a facilitator. An individual cannot be taught directly, but learning can be facilitated. This does not mean that there is no role for the teacher: clearly, there are times when information needs to be transmitted to pupils. But the emphasis in this view of learning is on self-direction and use of experience. Self-direction implies that the notion of a curriculum is not strongly emphasised in Rogers' view of learning, since what is learned is largely a matter for the learner to decide. However, Rogers argues that if content is dictated by the learner, learning is more likely to be long-lasting, since what is learned is in response to personal needs and goals. These are related to the experiential element of learning. Rogers contrasts experiential learning with what he calls cognitive or meaningless learning – when learning is related to academic tasks without any reference to the needs of the learner. According to Rogers, experiential learning has the following characteristics:

- there is personal involvement
- it is self initiated
- assessment is carried out via self evaluation on the part of the learner

The teacher as facilitator, ensures that the above characteristics are present in the learning encounter, by creating an appropriate and positive learning environment, and involves practical steps, such as having materials and resources available and taking *affective* steps such as paying attention to the *emotional* aspects of learning and being willing to share feelings and thoughts with pupils.

There is a temptation to view Rogers' theories as being out of tune with the current UK education system, where the emphases are on a largely prescribed curriculum and external measures of progress for individual pupils and for schools as a whole. Where in this system is there room for learning based on personal needs, self direction and facilitation rather than on teaching? Perhaps we should consider the interpersonal emphasis in Rogers' approach. Despite the imposition of curriculum content, teaching methodology and external performance benchmarks, the essence of teaching still involves interaction between an adult and a group of children or young people. Teachers – and teaching assistants – still need to be able to build relationships with pupils to bring out the best in them. Think about a subject you particularly enjoyed at school. The chances are that the teacher who taught you had something to do with your enjoyment and interest. This is where the interpersonal skills of adults who work in schools are vital to pupil engagement and motivation.

Summary

Experiential learning involves self-direction and views the teacher as a facilitator. The theories associated with this dimension of learning are more often in adult education than in school contexts. But there is a place for some consideration of the experiential dimension via the emphasis on interpersonal skills and the way in which these might contribute to success.

Reflection point

Pupil disaffection is a particular problem for secondary schools. Many pupils 'vote with their feet' or are disruptive in class as a response to an education system they perceive as irrelevant.

How could a Rogerian perspective on education help to reduce pupil disaffection?

The experiential dimension view of Jennifer

There are a number of factors in Jennifer's difficulties that the *experiential* dimension would identify. These are as follows:

- Jennifer isn't a self directed learner
- the learning offered has little personal meaning for her

If you were the teaching assistant working with Jennifer, how useful are the above points in helping you to deal with Jennifer's difficulties more effectively? Rate their usefulness on a scale of nought to ten, nought being not at all useful and ten being very useful. Make a note of your ratings, as we will ask you to compare them all after you have finished Part 3.

The intelligence dimension

Part 3 of this book has been concerned with learning. We have examined a number of views about learning under the umbrella term 'dimension'. This final section of Part Three looks at some of the ideas that underpin views of learning. Whatever view or theory about learning is discussed, there is an assumption that we know what we mean by the ability to learn. The word often used to describe this ability to learn is *intelligence*.

Before tackling the subject of intelligence in depth, it is important to consider this notion carefully. The box on page 140 has a suggestion for how you might start.

Our point is that we all have notions about intelligence, but that we might not use that particular term. Sometimes we use the word 'bright' instead. It is often used when a pupil isn't doing well at school and we express our surprise by saying that she or he is 'bright'. This implies that there are other aspects of learning besides those the child is taught in school. Perhaps we are talking about an ability to learn, rather than the specific skills or knowledge that are taught. When we talk about potential, are we saying that we can predict how far a child will be

What do you think about intelligence?

To start you thinking, we want you to consider two common comments that you have probably heard in the staff room or even made yourself. They are:

'S/he's very bright'

'S/he has a lot of potential'

What exactly is meant by these comments? How would you define 'bright' and 'potential' if challenged?

How would your colleagues define these terms?

Do you think you would agree?

able to go in terms of learning? How do we know? At the beginning of part three, learning was broadly defined as involving change. The specifics of the change are to be found in the theories associated with each of the dimensions examined in this part of the book.

In the innate ability dimension, there is not a view or theory about the type of change that occurs as a result of learning. Rather, this dimension is concerned with the fact that all humans have the ability and potential to learn and, therefore, to change. However, we do not learn and change in a uniform way. There is a huge variety in the attainments of individuals. Theories about intelligence also involve a consideration of individual differences. Why does person A become a nuclear physicist and person B a road sweeper? Is it related to their innate ability to learn, the premise being that the nuclear physicist is more capable of learning than the road sweeper? Or is it related to the life chances that have been available to each individual? Of course it could also be argued that both individuals are capable of becoming nuclear physicists but that only one of them chose to do so. Issues about value are also part of our examination of these two individuals. In contrasting a nuclear physicist and a road sweeper, I have assumed that the former is of more value than the latter. Certainly it is highly likely that the nuclear physicist will be paid more than the road sweeper. In our Western culture, we tend to place high value on academic and so called intellectual achievements, although this is not always reflected in monetary terms: think about the amount of money earned by professional footballers, many of whom will have only been educated up to the statutory school leaving age of sixteen. However, does this mean that a professional footballer is less intelligent than the nuclear physicist? It could be argued that the ability to earn vast sums of money and to manage that money, takes some kind of ability. The debate about what constitutes intelligence is the first issue that we will consider.

Secondly, we will look at the measurement of intelligence. This is an area of continuing heated debate and controversy. It is also an area that will have a profound impact on how we make judgements about pupil attainment and progress.

What is intelligence?

In part three we looked at a number of dimensions related to learning and found that, within a broad definition of learning, related to the idea of change, each dimension has its distinct perspective on the nature of the change that takes place as a result of learning. If we accept the notion of some kind of general underlying ability that all humans possess, we can look at a number of different emphases made by each dimension. The table below suggests what these might be:adapts to the environment.

Dimension	Suggested emphasis
Biological	General ability is a biological mechanism and heredity plays a large part in determining its level. The biological element means that general ability is thought to be fixed, thus setting the limits for what an individual can be expected to achieve.
Behavioural	General ability determines the extent of the success with which the individual adapts to the environment.
Instructional	General ability is the ability to profit from instruction and the notion that cognitive functions can be taught.
Social constructivist	General ability involves a set of cognitive functions that are not thought to be fixed. Therefore, these functions can be taught. General ability is related to flexibility of thought.
Experiential	General ability comprises the thinking skills needed in order to reflect on experience.

The definition of intelligence found in Webster's Dictionary encompasses most of the above:

> The ability to learn or understand or to deal with new or trying situations. The skilled use of reason. The ability to apply knowledge to manipulate one's environment or to think abstractly as measured by objective criteria (tests).

Edward Boring, an American psychologist, observed in the 1920s that intelligence is what is measured by intelligence tests! The notion of what is meant by intelligence is often overshadowed by the measurement industry, and it is tempting to accept Boring's definition. When 'bright' is used as a description of a pupil, we consider that this describes a pupil who is able to learn, but that being 'bright' did not necessarily relate to success in school subjects. Therefore, the notion of intelligence is something to do with the *process* of learning, rather than the *product*. The measurement of intelligence is only one part of the whole area of intelligence and is called *psychometrics,* discussed on page 144.

Intelligence remains a subject of intense debate within psychology. Just as definitions of learning vary according to the school of psychology, the same is true of intelligence. The underlying idea of what constitutes intelligence is a notion that humans possess some kind of generalised ability that is not linked to particular skills or achievements. This general ability is the subject of debate, giving rise to questions such as: does it exist? is it inherited? does environment play a part? One of the major debates in the field of intelligence is the nature/nurture debate, the extent to which intelligence is inherited or develops as a result of exposure to the environment. We have already considered this debate at the beginning of this section, the biological dimension and in the language acquisition and development section of part two. Historically, intelligence has been viewed as mainly due to inherited factors. Evidence to back up this claim has been derived from twin studies. Proponents of the inheritance theory suggest that identical twins separated at birth, and therefore brought up in different environments, show the same levels of intelligence. Although there is some evidence, there are insufficient studies to make this link conclusive. One of the most well known researchers into the heritability of intelligence was the British psychologists Sir Cyril Burt. Burt was the first psychologist to be employed by a local education authority and as such is considered to be the first educational psychologist. His work about intelligence led to the use of the eleven plus test as a means of selecting children for grammar schools. Burt carried out work on identical twins separated at birth and claimed that the consistency in his results demonstrated that intelligence was inherited. Some years after his death, it was found that he had forged results in order to strengthen the evidence for his claims.

This introduction highlights two things. First, that there is no universal agreement about the nature of intelligence, and secondly, that our views about teaching and learning are shaped by our view of the nature of intelligence. For example, if we are convinced that intelligence is fixed and that our potential is determined by our genes, we may view learning failure as the child's problem, not ours; the child simply isn't intelligent enough to benefit from teaching.

The subject of intelligence tends to be dominated by the science and industry of its measurement. We will look at this aspect of the subject later. However, some theories of intelligence are not related to measurement. One of the areas of study for cognitive psychology is that of mental processes. Rather than measure these processes and then call them intelligence, these approaches are more concerned with identifying the process skills underlying the ability to learn. We will also look at this aspect of the subject. Before moving on to look both these points, take time to complete the activity in the box below. It is important that you reflect on where you stand in relation to some of these issues and theories because your views are likely to influence how you deal with your pupils.

Reflection point: your views about intelligence

As we have seen, there is no universally accepted definition of intelligence. It is important for you to think about where you stand, as your views about this subject are likely to influence the way in which you deal with the pupils in your care.

Below are a number of statements about the nature of intelligence, based on the material in the first paragraphs of this section. Read each statement, then write your assessment of each statement on the scale below, choosing a position that shows how much you agree or disagree with each statement. If possible, it would be useful to do this with a colleague and compare your results.

■ intelligence is fixed

■ intelligence is mainly down to heredity

■ intelligence is about abstract thinking

■ intelligence is about learning how to learn

■ intelligence is a set of specific abilities that can be measured

■ some people are more intelligent than others

■ intelligence can be improved

■ intelligence is about being able to learn from experience (some people just never do!)

■ intelligence is about adaptability

■ intelligence is being able to reason and think abstractly

1	5	10
Agree strongly	Neither agree nor disagree	Disagree strongly

Now look at your completed scale.

What does it tell you about your view of intelligence?

To what extent do your views affect the way you view the attainments and progress of the pupils with whom you work?

Measuring intelligence

One of the reasons why intelligence is the subject of intense debate is related to views about the measurement of intelligence. The idea that the general ability of individuals, however we define it, can be measured is called *psychometrics*. Psychometrics is the science of psychological measurement. A psychometric view of intelligence comprises the identification of a set of specific mental or cognitive abilities that can be measured. The measurement of these abilities involves a comparison with age-related norms that are created using the tests with samples from the population to determine the average score for particular ages. It is then possible to examine the results and determine whether the individual tested is average, above average or below average for their age. The way in which intelligence is measured today harks back to developments in psychology in the early twentieth century. Although the content of tests has changed over the years to prevent individuals failing because of unfamiliarity with the context, the basic methodology and principles have changed little over the past hundred years. The basic principles are as follows:

- there are specific skills which indicate the extent of the presence of underlying general ability

- it is possible to measure these skills

- it is possible to express the measurement of underlying ability as an IQ score. An IQ score is derived from a comparison of mental age and chronological age. Mental age is determined by the level of performance on the tasks in the test. For example, a child aged twelve years who performed at the level of a nine year old would be said to have a mental age of nine. The IQ is then calculated as follows:

$$\frac{\text{Mental age} \times 100}{\text{Chronological age}}$$

Intelligence tests used today rarely give a mental age for an individual, but they do give an IQ score. IQ scores have always been thought to follow the so called *Bell Curve*, or normal distribution. Normal distribution means that most people's IQ scores would fall in the middle and the scores rise and fall at an equal rate from the average. The Bell Curve is illustrated opposite.

The measurement of intelligence is rooted in historical developments in psychology. The section below gives a brief historical overview, illustrating how these developments are still present in the measurement of intelligence today.

Historical overview

Francis Galton was an English academic and cousin of Charles Darwin. Galton made the first studies of individual differences. His book *Hereditary Genius* was

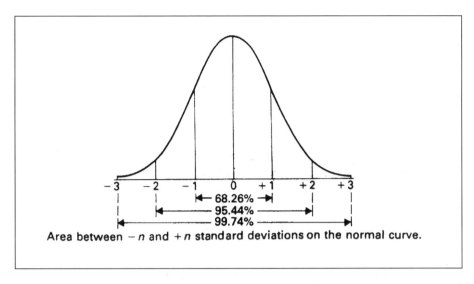

Area between − *n* and + *n* standard deviations on the normal curve.

published in 1869. Galton thought that individual differences were a matter of inheritance. He was the first individual to take a scientific approach to the measurement of individual ability. Previous studies in this area were in the realm of *phrenology,* which is the study of the shape and size of the head as an indicator of intellectual ability. Galton devised tests of motor and sensory skills as indicators of an individual's overall ability. He also devised statistical methods which are still used today and was the first person to apply the bell curve of normal distribution to individual differences.

Galton's theories about individual differences also contained ideas that are considered highly controversial and offensive today. He used his ideas about individual differences to rank populations and asserted that African people were mentally inferior to Anglo-Saxon people. These notions about individual difference were responsible for a growing interest in eugenics. Eugenics is defined in the Oxford Dictionary as 'improvement of the qualities of a race by control of inherited characteristics'. Eugenics involved selective breeding in order to achieve this goal. Taking the idea that intelligence is an inherited characteristic, eugenics would advocate selective breeding in order to produce a more intelligent population. So eugenics has sinister aspects. The idea that an improved population can be created can also lead to the destruction of populations who are perceived as inferior. This is the extreme to which the Nazis took the theory of eugenics, annihilating Jews as part of the Nazi programme to create an Aryan master race and also slaughtering the mentally and physically disabled.

This may seem interesting as a history lesson, but there is more. After Galton's initial attempts to measure intelligence and classify individuals, many other psychologists and scientists took to developing intelligence tests. Intelligence tests used today are still based on work carried out at the beginning of the twentieth century. Many of those involved in test development at that time were also heavily involved in the eugenics movement. The notion that some races are intellectually inferior to others has persisted. In the late 1960s, Arthur Jensen suggested that white children were more intelligent than black children. In 1995, a book by Herrnstein and Murray, *The Bell Curve: Intelligence and Class Structure in American Life* promoted views about the genetic inheritance of intelligence and argued that intelligence shows variations *between* ethnic groups as well as *within* ethnic groups, with African Americans overall showing lower scores in tests of intelligence than White Americans. In the UK Christopher Brand published *The g Factor* (1996), which argued that there were differences in intelligence between black populations and white. He was dismissed from his post at Edinburgh University and his book was subsequently withdrawn by its publisher, Wiley.

The next significant developments took place in the first quarter of the twentieth century. A French psychologist, **Alfred Binet**, developed a test to determine whether pupils were educable or not. The test distinguished between pupils who had behavioural difficulties and pupils who had *learning* difficulties, who in the terminology of the time, were 'mentally retarded'. Binet never intended his test to be used to rank pupils. He did not believe that intelligence was fixed and thought it could not be measured and given as a single score. Despite his views, his tests were developed by others, notably an American psychologist called Lewis Terman. Terman's work led to a version of Binet's test called the Stanford-Binet, as Terman worked at Stanford University. Interestingly, Terman was one of the psychologists who followed the eugenics movement. An updated form of the Stanford-Binet Test is still used today.

Charles Spearman proposed the idea of the *g* factor. He thought that intelligence comprised two elements. The *g* factor stood for general intelligence and could be found in all aspects of performance when completing an intelligence test. The second factor was the *s* or specific factor. This factor related to specific tests so that *g* is required to perform all tasks, whereas *s* is only required for some tasks. Spearman arrived at this notion after he carried out statistical analysis of scores from tests that measure intelligence: the technique he developed is called *factor analysis.* Although Spearman identified *g* by this statistical process, he was not very clear about what it was. He described it, rather vaguely, as 'mental energy'. The idea of the *g* factor persists in many views about and definitions of intelligence. These views all subscribe to the underlying notion that there is a series of inherent abilities that enable the individual to learn that are unrelated to the specific content of learning. Moreover, these views suggest that underlying abilities can be measured and the results used to comment on the individual's potential: that is, how much or to what extent the person is likely to profit from formal instruction. Measurement of these underlying abilities would help to predict the individual's future educational achievements. Many of these ideas arose as a result of Spearman's proposal of the existence of *g*.

David Wechsler was a student of Spearman. In 1939, Wechsler developed a test of intelligence. The Wechsler Intelligence Scale for Children (WISC) is one of the most commonly used IQ tests in current use. It consists of a number of sub-tests. These sub-tests measure verbal ability, the verbal scales, and non-verbal ability, the performance scales. Wechsler devised these scales and their subtests on the principle that intelligence consists of a series of skills or abilities. He defined intelligence as 'the capacity of a person to act purposefully, to think rationally and to deal effectively with his/her environment' (Wechsler, 1944).

The content of intelligence tests

Tests that set out to measure intelligence first determine the underlying skills and then devise a means of measuring them. These skills are usually measured separately, in a series of sub-tests. The pupil receives a score for each sub-test, based on the number of test items performed correctly. This is called a raw score. Raw scores are then converted into standardised scores. This is to enable a comparison to be made between the pupil's performance with that of other pupils of the same age. In order to be able to make this comparison, intelligence tests are standardised. This means that a sample of the population for whom the test is designed is taken and the test is administered. The purpose of the standardisation is to arrive at what is considered to be an average performance. It is assumed that the Bell Curve represents the normal distribution of intelligence so that in devising an IQ test, the results obtained from a sample should reflect this normal distribution. The process of standardisation sets out to do just this. Tests are piloted with to make sure that they are reliable and valid. A reliable test means that the same results would be obtained on repeated administration. A valid test means that the test measures what it says it will measure. Sometimes raw scores are also converted into percentile scores. A percentile score gives the individual's position in a cross section of one hundred children the same age. A percentile score of 100 is the highest and 50 represents an average performance. In contrast, a standardised score of 100 represents an average performance. Many intelligence tests measure verbal IQ and performance IQ. This means that there are two distinct sets of subtests; one set that measures verbal abilities and one set that measures non verbal abilities. The score from both sets of sub-tests can be combined to obtain a score for a full scale IQ; that is, an IQ score that takes account of both verbal and non-verbal performance.

Two tests that are most commonly used by educational psychologists: the Wechsler Intelligence Scale for Children (WISC) and the British Ability Scales (BAS).

The WISC was developed by David Wechsler, discussed above. His test sets out to measure intelligence via a series of subtests devised to reflect the range of intellectual abilities that the individual might possess. Although this test will give an IQ score, the manual for the WISC advises practitioners that the scores derived from the sub-tests do not necessarily represent everything we know and can measure in relation to intelligence: 'While the intellectual abilities represented in the scale may be essential as precursors of intelligent behaviour, other determinants of intelligence, non-intellectual in nature, also help to determine how a child's abilities are expressed. These factors, which are not so much skills as traits and attitudes, are not directly tapped by standardised measures of intellectual ability, yet they influence children's performance on these measures as well as their effectiveness in daily living and life's wider challenges' (*WISC Manual,* 1992).

The British Ability Scales (Elliot, 1997) measures 'general cognitive ability' (GCA), rather than IQ. It is based on the notion of *g*, the underlying factor in intelligence identified by Spearman. In the BAS manual, *g* is defined thus: 'psychometric *g* is the general ability of an individual to perform complex mental processing that involves conceptualisation and the transformation of information'. The BAS prefers to refer to GCA rather than IQ because the authors feel that intelligence can be defined in a number of different ways, causing confusion about what exactly is being measured. The emphasis in the BAS is on measures of *g* that can give a picture of overall intellectual functioning. The BAS includes three achievement scales, which measure performance in specific curriculum content areas: number skills, spelling and word reading. Scores from the achievement scales are not used to calculate the GCA, but can be used as a comparative measure. It is possible to analyse differences between GCA scores and achievement scores to suggest when a child is underachieving.

The table opposite shows the content of WISC and BAS subtests. It summarises the skill or ability measured by the sub-test and, where appropriate, shows equivalent sub-tests in the WISC and BAS.

Measuring intelligence: issues to consider
The measurement of intelligence is based on a number of assumptions. First, it is assumed that the skills sampled actually constitute intelligence. Secondly, it is assumed that there is a normal distribution of scores. Thirdly, it is assumed that the skills that are being measured are universal. There are three significant problems with these assumptions:

■ how do we know that the skills being sampled constitute intelligence? The fact is, we do not know for sure. The skills that are measured have been identified via statistical analysis of people's performance and are still

SKILL OR ABILITY	WISC SUBTEST	BAS SUBTEST
Knowledge of facts, knowledge about people, places, objects and events	Information	
Understanding of language. The WISC subtest also involves problem solving about everyday events, that involve knowledge of social rules	Comprehension	
Expressive language, definitions of words	Vocabulary	Word definitions
Concepts about number	Arithmetic	Number skills
Verbal reasoning and categorising: being able to say how two things are alike (for example, a dog and a cat are both animals)	Similarities	Verbal similarities
Identifying a missing part from a picture. Involves visual discrimination and comparison	Picture completion	
Arranging a set of pictures in a logical order, using sequencing and ordering skills	Picture arrangement	
Spatial awareness, visual and motor skills	Block design	Pattern construction
Spatial awareness, visual and motor skills. Perceptual skills: being able to visualise the whole thing when given the parts	Object assembly	
Speed with which information is processed	Coding	Speed of information processing
Non verbal reasoning, deducing relationships		Matrices
Identifying and applying rules, knowledge of numerical relationships		Quantitative reasoning
Short term visual memory		Recognition of pictures

based on Spearman's notion, which is nearly a hundred years old, that there is a *g* factor. There is no irrefutable evidence for the existence of *g*

■ how do we know that the normal distribution applies? In fact, there is evidence that IQ scores are increasing. This is called the Flynn effect after the psychologist James Flynn. If IQ is not distributed according to the *Bell Curve*, we cannot make a judgment about who is above or below average

---

Reflection point: measuring intelligence

Rosenthal and Jacobson looked at what happened when teachers were led to believe that their pupils were high or low achievers. They told teachers that they had carried out an IQ test, and as a result had identified pupils who would make 'dramatic intellectual growth'. In fact, there was no IQ test and the pupils had been selected randomly. After a period of a few months, the pupils who had been identified as the high achievers had shown improvements, whereas the pupils not identified as high achievers had not shown improvements. Teachers of the so called 'high achievers' group behaved differently. They spent more time with the pupils and showed more enthusiasm about teaching them. They described these pupils as being better behaved and more curious and interested.

Rosenthal commented about this research:

> Superb teachers can teach the unteachable, we know that. So, what I think this research shows is that there's a moral obligation for a teacher: if the teacher knows that certain students can't learn, that teacher should get out of that classroom.

This was a powerful piece of research.

Do you think this still happens today?

Think about the reflection point at the beginning of this section. You were asked to think about the word 'bright'. Write down five characteristics of bright pupils. Now write down five characteristics of pupils who are 'not bright'.

How do you know that the pupils you think of as bright really are bright? What would happen if you treated all pupils as if they were bright?

We might say 'I treat all pupils the same.' Is this *really* true? How can we be sure?

(Rosenthal and Jacobson, 1968)

■ these skills have not been proven to be universal. The problem lies with standardisation procedures. Often tests are standardised with a particular section of the population. In the past, this has tended to be a white European population. If tests are only used with white European individuals, it could be argued that the results would be valid. Unfortunately, this is not the case. On numerous occasions, IQ tests are administered to individuals from ethnic groups with whom the tests have not been standardised. Therefore, when judgments are made about the individual's IQ, a like-for-like comparison is not being made. Similarly, it can be argued that using these tests with individuals for whom English is an additional language will produce similarly skewed results. The problem here is not the fact that the tests have not been standardised on a range of populations, but that the results are used to judge and classify individuals *despite* this fact. Ethnicity is not the only factor. There is also an issue about the validity of carrying out an IQ test with a hearing impaired pupil who communicates via sign language, or with a visually-impaired pupil

In thinking about whether use of measures of IQ are appropriate or useful, we should also consider the historical roots of this testing. Think back to the historical overview. The measurement of intelligence has strong links with *eugenics*. Is this appropriate in a 21st century multiracial society?

The contribution of cognitive psychology: other views of intelligence

Most psychologists would agree that individuals possess underlying abilities that help us to learn. Much of the controversy in the field of intelligence arises when we begin to try to measure these abilities and to classify pupils on the basis of these measurements. The previous section has illustrated the enormous difficulties involved in attempting to measure and classify.

Aside from this debate, other psychologists have attempted to suggest the nature of these underlying abilities to give some insight into what is involved in the process of becoming a learner. There are many views about this. For the purposes of this section, the work of two psychologists, Howard Gardner and Robert Sternberg is explained.

Howard Gardner proposed the idea of 'multiple intelligences'. He rejects the notion that intelligence can be attributed to one factor (the g factor) and instead suggests that there are a number of independent factors, or cognitive abilities, that make up intelligence:

■ linguistic
■ musical

- logical/mathematical
- spatial
- bodily/kinaesthetic (control of the body and skilful movement)
- intrapersonal (understanding one's own thoughts and behaviour)
- interpersonal (relating to others, understanding their feelings)

Robert Sternberg proposed the idea of triarchic intelligence: that there are three main underlying abilities: analytical, creative and practical. Analytical intelligence involves the ability to solve puzzles and use analogical thought. Creative intelligence involves the ability to cope with new situations. Practical intelligence involves the ability to solve real-life problems. Sternberg does not disagree with the notion of measuring intelligence, but rejects the idea of IQ tests on the basis that the skills and abilities sampled are too narrow. He comments that our society values the prediction of achievements rather than the achievements themselves. He feels that IQ alone is not sufficient for predicting success. He defines intelligence as 'the cognitive ability of an individual to learn from experience, to reason well, to remember important information and to cope with the demands of daily living'. Sternberg has developed the Adaptive Behaviour Checklist, which is a series of skills related to the three aspects of intelligence. This checklist can be used to identify skills already evident and those that need to be learned, as Sternberg does not subscribe to the notion that intelligence is fixed – although in common with many psychologists, he acknowledges that a small percentage of intelligence is attributable to genetic factors.

Summary

This final section of Part 3 contains the most controversial issues. The notion of intelligence is not something that can be easily defined or observed which is why many assumptions are made about it. Even though intelligence is based on a number of assumptions, an entire industry in the intelligence testing has developed over the years. Despite reservations, measures of IQ are still made and an individual is classified or labelled according to these measurements. What seems to have been forgotten are the links between the measurement of intelligence and the eugenics movement. Concerns about the relevance of IQ tests for populations for which the tests have not been standardised have not halted their use. The organisations and individuals that are responsible for test development should not be held solely responsible for their continuation. It is clear from a scrutiny of the manuals for the WISC and BAS that the test authors do not think that scores from the tests tell us everything we need to know about an individual. Both tests acknowledge their limitations and do not measure factors such as motivation, persistence or impulsiveness. And the BAS manual makes a clear statement about the idea of potential:

...ability test scores cannot be appropriately interpreted as setting the upper limit, or ceiling, of a child's future performance. Such negative used of the term potential is unjustified and may be harmful.

The notes of caution in the tests manuals might indicate that misuse of IQ and intelligence tests lies with those using the tests, not with the tests themselves. The BAS manual suggests that the most useful and appropriate method of assessment is a mixture of data about cognitive abilities, such as would be measured by the BAS or WISC, together with criterion referenced data:

these approaches [cognitive and behavioural] are not mutually exclusive and a mixture of the two approaches is arguably the best possible form of practice.

This might seem quite a depressing picture. Although the psychometric element of intelligence is still powerful, other notions are being recognised increasingly as an alternative to IQ measurement and subsequent classification. There seems no doubt that a range of skills and abilities exist which help us to be effective learners. These are called *cognitive* abilities, or thinking skills. Over the past five to ten years, there has been increased interest in these skills, as there has been a recognition that the processes of learning are just as important as the content. After many years of emphasising content, the National Curriculum now acknowledges that process skills are important. Helping pupils to learn effectively means that they are more likely to benefit from curriculum content. In 1998 a project was commissioned by the Government in order to look at the role of cognitive abilities. The National Curriculum now contains guidance about the process skills needed to access curriculum content.

In addition to the initiatives related specifically to the National Curriculum, other cognitive education programmes are receiving wider recognition. The work of Reuven Feurstein is becoming known to a larger audience (the social constructivist dimension). His experiences and ideas, described earlier, provide a powerful argument for disregarding the outcomes of IQ tests. The teaching programmes arising from Feurstein's work 'Instrumental Enrichment' and 'Bright Start' demonstrate that individuals can be taught to be more effective thinkers and as a result can achieve greater success in life.

The words of Robert Sternberg given in an interview to *Skeptic* magazine, available on the internet, appropriately conclude this section:

There is no absolute agreed-on definition of intelligence. One of the battles in the field, arguably the battle, even more than the heredity-environment issue is, what you include under the definition of intelligence. There's no final answer because God doesn't tell us what he means. To a large extent, intelligence is our own creation ... To me, something is a part of intelligence if it's necessary for adaptation.

The intelligence dimension view of Jennifer

There are a number of factors in Jennifer's difficulties that the *innate ability* dimension would identify:

- ■ her learning difficulties are due to low intelligence

- ■ she probably inherited her low intelligence from her mum

If you were the teaching assistant working with Jennifer, how useful would the above emphases be in helping you to intervene in Jennifer's difficulties more effectively? Rate their usefulness on a scale of nought to ten, nought being not at all useful and ten being very useful. Make a note of your ratings, as we will ask you to compare them all after you have finished Part 3.

Conclusion to Part 3

As you have seen, there are many different ways of looking at children's learning. There are no right or wrong answers to the question 'how do we learn?' However, each perspective will have various levels of usefulness when applied to the pupils that you work with on a day-to-day basis.

At the beginning of Part 3 we introduced you to Jennifer. At the end of each section, we suggested the way in which each of the dimensions of learning might interpret or view her difficulties. You were asked to think about these views in relation to their usefulness. Now we would like you to summarise your thoughts and ratings. The purpose of this final activity is to help you to reflect on any theories of learning on which you might base your practice and to make informed choices when you are trying to intervene in a pupil's difficulties. An understanding of why these difficulties occur is likely to help you to suggest appropriate intervention.

Therefore, as a concluding activity to Part 3, fill in the table on pages 155 and 156 and then do the application activity on page 157.

Dimension	View of learning	Explanation of difficulties	Implications for intervention	Your rating	Your comments
Biological	Changes that take place as a result of learning are related to neurological factors	Learning difficulties attributed to neurological defects or deficiencies	We use interventions that aim to make or improve neurological connections or to link up the two hemispheres of the brain		
Behavioural	Learning is a change in observable behaviour and is influenced by antecedents and consequences	Need to adjust curriculum so that small changes can be observed. Look at changing antecedents so that conditions for learning are right	We task analyse the curriculum and use behavioural objectives so we are clear about the changes we want to see. We change antecedents if necessary (for example, seating)		
Instructional	Learning occurs as a result of instruction and is therefore dependent on the quality and appropriateness of instruction	If learning has not occurred then neither has teaching. Instruction might be inappropriate	We make changes to instruction: for example, the size, pace and type. We find out what teaches best by using evaluation methods such as Precision Teaching		
Social constructivist	Learning is related to social factors and is an active, interactive process that involves meaning and understanding. It takes place when a mediator is present in order to help the learner make sense of stimuli. It involves cognitive functions and processes rather than content	Learning difficulties are due to inadequate development of the necessary cognitive functions (thinking skills) that are needed to access curriculum content and to a lack of mediation of these functions	We mediate to the pupil. We teach the cognitive functions needed to access content; that is, we emphasise process not content		

Dimension	View of learning	Explanation of difficulties	Implications for intervention	Your rating	Your comments
Experiential	Learning is related to personal change and comes about as a result of the individual reflecting on experience	Learning difficulties are due to a lack of self direction and the fact that the learning offered has little personal meaning	We give more choice and plan a curriculum that has personal meaning		
Intelligence	Learning is a series of skills and abilities that are innate. We call these intelligence	Difficulties in learning are due to the individual having low intelligence	If we view intelligence as fixed there is little we can do by way of intervention, except to make sure that we take account of ability levels and IQ when we decide what to present to pupils		

Application

Throughout Part 3, we have applied theories of learning to our fictitious pupil, Jennifer. Now that you have worked through each section in relation to a fictitious pupil, you can now begin to apply your knowledge to a real pupil.

Write a brief profile of a pupil you work with. Use the profile of Jennifer if you want a framework for the sort of information to include. Then look in detail at the pupil's learning difficulties and decide which of the dimensions will help you to plan the next steps of learning. You do not need to select just one; there might be several that are helpful to you. Now plan the next steps of learning for this pupil and decide how you are going to evaluate progress.

References and further reading

Association of American Educators (1988) *Project Follow Through*

Ausubel, D (1978) *Educational Psychology: A Cognitive View (2nd Edition)* New York: Holt, Reinhart and Winston.

Baddeley, A (1999) *Essentials of Human Memory* London: Psychology Press

Bereiter, C and Engelmann, S (1966) *Teaching Disadvantaged Children* Engelwood Cliffs NJ: Prentice Hall Inc

Binet, A and Simon, T (1905) Methode nouvelles pour le diagnostic du niveau intellectuel des anormaux. *L'Annee Psychologique*, 11, 191-336

Bruner, J (1973) *Going Beyond the Information Given.* New York: Norton.

Dennison, P. and Dennison, G (1994) *Brain Gym.* Ventura CA: Edu-Kinesthetic

Elliot, Colin D (1983) *The British Ability Scales.* Windsor: NFER Nelson

Engelmann, S and Carnine, D (1991) *Theory of Instruction: Principles and Applications.* Eugene OR: ADI Press

Feurstein, R, Feurstein, R S, Falik, L H and Rand Y (2002) *The Dynamic Assessment of Cognitive Modifiability.* Jerusalem: ICELP Press.

Flynn, J (1984) *The Mean IQ of Americans: Massive Gains.* New York: Harper and Row

Galton, F (1883) *Inquiries into Human Faculty and its Development.* London: Macmillan

Gardner, H. (1983) *Frames of Mind: The theory of multiple intelligence.* New York: Basic Books

Haring, N, G Lovitt, T C, Eaton, M D and Hansen, C L (1978). *The Fourth R: Research in the Classroom.* Columbus OH: Merrill.

Hayward, H Carl and Brooks, P (1992) *Bright Start Cognitive Curriculum for Young Children.* Watertown: Charlesbridge Publishing

Herrnstein, R and Murray. C (1994) *The Bell Curve: Intelligence and Class Structure in American Life.* NY: The Free Press.

Jensen, A (1973) *Educational Differences.* New York: Routeledge and Kegan Paul

Lindsley, O R (1990) *Precision Teaching: By Teachers for Children. Exceptional Children,* 22 (3) 10-15

Mager, R (1962) *Preparing Instructional Objectives.* Belmont CA: Lake Publishing Co.

Perfetti, C (1979) Levels of language and levels of process. In: L. Cermak and F. Craik (Eds). *Levels of processing in human memory.* Hillsdale NJ: Erlbaum.

Rogers, C (1969) *Freedom to Learn*. Columbus OH: Merrill

Rosenthal, R and Jacobson, L (1968) *Pygmalion in the Classroom: Teacher expectation and pupils' intellectual development*. New York: Holt, Rinehart and Winston.

Skinner, B F (1974) *About Behavioris*. New York: Knopf.

Smith, A (1998) *Accelerated Learning in Practice*. Stafford: Network Educational Press

Spearman, C A (1927) *The Abilities of Man*. London: Macmillan.

Sternberg, R (1985) *Beyond IQ: A Triarchic Theory of Human Intelligence*. New York: Cambridge University Press

Terman, L (1916) *The Measurement of Intelligence*. Boston: Houghton Muffin

Vygotsky, L S (1978) *Mind in Society Cambridge*. Massachusetts: Harvard University Press.

Wechsler, D (1939) *The Measurement of Adult Intelligence*. NY: Williams and Williams

Wheldall, K and Glynn, T (1989) *Effective Classroom Learning*. Oxford: Blackwell.

Part 4
The Psychology of Groups and Institutions

8

Processes in Groups

This chapter

■ examines the influence of other people on individual behaviour

■ describes the stages in the development of groups

■ describes the different roles that can be taken in successful and productive groups

Group influence on individual social behaviour

All the different schools of psychology agree on the importance of the social nature of human beings. We live in the most sophisticated and biggest group of large animals on the planet. The ability to work in groups has contributed to the success of our species. Understanding the psychological processes which take place in human groups offers insight into the way in which being with other people influences the ways that we behave, think and speak. As teaching assistants, you will be part of a number of different groups, including classes, staff meetings, case conferences and reviews. We begin with some famous studies in *cognitive* psychology.

Compliance

Imagine yourself in a group of strangers. The group is asked to observe an object. What do the other members of the group say? You are the last to report, but the other members of the group say something quite different from what you were going to say. It gets to your turn. What do you do? Do you say what you were going to say, or go along with the views of the other group members. This was the issue researched by Raymond Asch in a series of important experiments.

Asch arranged for a group of seven people to take part in an experiment. Unknown to the seventh person in the group, the other six were actors. The subjects were told that the experiment was looking at visual perception – how we see things. The group was presented with pictures of three lines of different lengths. A fourth line was presented and the group was asked to indicate which of the first three lines were the same length as the fourth. Unknown to the real subject, the actors lied, all agreeing that one of the other lines was the same length. As you might expect, the real subject was influenced by the presence and behaviour of the others.

The results were interesting:

- over one third of the responses always agreed (conformed) with the views of the actors

- three quarters of the subjects conformed to the views of the actors at least once

- there were considerable individual differences. One quarter of the subjects did not agree (conform) at any stage. The subjects felt tension and anxiety during the process

- when the experiment was repeated with dissenting views, the results changed again. If just one of the actors dissented, the conformity went down from 32 per cent to 6 per cent

Question: Have you ever experienced pressure from a group to conform? Have you ever changed what you have said in a group in the light of what the majority have said?

Obedience to authority

Asch's work relates to people behaving in a way which keeps them in some kind of group, perhaps it reflects a tendency to want to feel comfortable. By contrast, we consider the famous work of Stanley Milgram. He looked at the extent to which we are prepared to harm other people because we are told to do so by an authority figure.

Milgram, like Asch used actors. He told the subject that he was researching the effects of punishment on learning. Two people the real subject and the actor were given roles. The actor was to be the person learning, and the real subject would be the person asking the questions and administering the punishment. The actor was taken into a room and strapped into a chair. Electrodes were attached to his wrists. A large volt meter indicated the voltage that would be administered to the actor when he got the answers wrong. The voltage indicated on the meter increased to a maximum of 450 volts. The real subject was told that no organic long-term harm would result from the person being shocked. No electricity at all was administered to the actor, but the subject did not know this. As the experiment progressed, the 'voltage' increased and the actor screamed with greater and greater force. The question under examination was, at what 'voltage' would the questioner stop?

The predictions were that people would begin to cease administering the shock after about 60 volts and that by 250 volts only one third would be prepared to continue. The actual results were very different. All the subjects went over 300 volts. Over half were prepared to administer the maximum of 450 volts. When the subjects were debriefed they reported feeling distress and tension, whether or not they continued to 450 volts. The fact remained that the majority continued to administer the shocks to the maximum level.

What factors led the subjects to carry on? The experiments were conducted in a well-established research lab in Yale. When the experiment was repeated in a run-down set of offices the obedience rate dropped to 48 per cent. There was an authority figure nearby, encouraging the subject to carry on. The obedience rate reduced to 21 per cent if the instructions to carry on were given by phone. There was generally a wall separating the subject from the actor. The obedience reduced from 65 per cent to 40 per cent if the subject was in the same room as the actor.

This experiment was criticised for a number of reasons: The way the experiment was set up which was artificial and did not reflect a real situation. Another experiment was set up to examine this. It was to find out to what extent nurses would obey an instruction which conflicted with the usual practice of a hospital.

Nurses were telephoned by a doctor they knew to be on the staff, but whom they had not met. They were instructed to give a patient a medicine from their medicine cabinet. The label of the medicine bottle indicated that the maximum daily dose was ten mg. They were asked to give the patient twenty mg. The doctor said that they would go to the ward in a short time to sign the order. The order conflicted with a number of hospital rules: The dose was excessive. The order should not have been given over the phone. The medicine was not on the regular list used by the ward the name was made up. Medicines should not be given without a signature. In spite of all these factors, a startling 95 per cent of nurses started to give the medication (which was actually a harmless tablet known as a placebo). This experiment made the Milgram study looked more convincing.

Deindividuation

The third effect researched is what leads people in groups to behave as if they were less responsible for their actions than if they were on their own. The situation most often referred to was the brutal murder of a woman in the street outside her home in New York. The murder took over half an hour to complete and in spite of extensive cries for help, no one came to her assistance. No-one even called the police. This phenomenon was called *bystander apathy*. Experiments were constructed to examine it. Latane and Darley devised an interesting situation. Some people were sitting in a room waiting for an interview. The room began to fill with smoke. The reactions of the subjects varied. If they were on their own, 75 per cent reported the smoke within two minutes. If they were there in a group of three, fewer than 13 per cent reported the smoke within the six minutes of the experiment. The subjects behaved as if the responsibility for reporting the smoke was shared between them and nobody actually took responsibility for the action. Other studies have supported this idea.

College students were invited to take part in a group discussion. The discussion took place via an intercom. One of the voices reported having a seizure. The question being considered was the extent to which participants reported the seizure. If the subjects believed they were on their own, 85 per cent reported it. Of those who believed they were in a group of three, 62 per cent reported it. If they believed they were in a group of six, only 31 per cent reported the event. The researchers developed the concept of the 'diffusion of responsibility'. The larger the group, the less we feel personally responsible for events that occur, however hazardous they may be.

How might these four studies apply to the work of teaching assistants?

You are at a meeting to review the educational progress of a child with some kind of special need. At the meeting there is a medical doctor, a psychologist, the teacher, teaching assistant and the child's mother. A problem is raised by the school. The doctor suggests that it might be better for the child to be educated in a special unit. The parent doesn't want her child to be removed from his current school. The doctor suggests the unit, the psychologist agrees. Consider the pressures on the parent. This situation combines compliance with obedience to authority and diffusion of responsibility. However, the teaching assistant can make a difference to the likelihood of the parent being able to express her views by not conforming to the views of the doctor and psychologist, if they think differently.

Applications of psychodynamic theories to groups

There are other schools of psychology which have important contributions to make to the understanding of the behaviour of people in groups. The *psychodynamic* school has looked at groups. One of the leading thinkers was Bion who developed the concept of *unconscious motivation* of a group. He suggests that there are two agendas operating in groups:

- the overt and conscious agenda which includes the tasks for the group and the reason for the existence of the group

- the hidden agenda of the group. This includes the life cycle of the group, unconscious processes occurring in the group including the emotions, motivations, and tensions – the defence mechanisms of the group

To illustrate some of these ideas let us consider some common phenomena in work groups.

Denial

One defence mechanism is to pretend that the events causing anxiety are simply not happening. Ofsted inspections are a source of great anxiety for staff in schools. One defence against that anxiety is to deny that the inspection matters. This could be articulated by staff saying they don't care about the inspection. 'What do they know about teaching?'

Cynicism

Staff may suggest that the motives of the inspectors are suspect. It's all political really. They are just doing it for the money etc.

Projection

This term relates to the psychological process in which people translate or *project* the source of anxiety on to some other object or person. Staff may find someone to blame for any negative comments made by the inspectors. Thoughts might include:

It's all because X is in my class
If only that child had been away that week, the report would have been different
The school is badly run
It's all the headteacher's fault
If only there were more resources

There are other possible examples, but the common threads are the concepts of the emotions present in groups and the existence of defence mechanisms.

The appeal of the psychodynamic analysis of the group behaviour lies in its ability to look at established groups, rather than those found in the transient groups used in the cognitive studies, however many groups found in education are not long-lived. Think about the group of people who meet to discuss a child who is causing concern. The following section considers groups as having their own developmental stages.

Stages in group development

The psychologist, Tuckman, examined evidence that groups have common features. He suggested that there were distinct stages in the way groups developed. He described five of these:

1. **Forming**

   When groups of people come together for the first time, there is a sense of insecurity. The members rely on old and polite ways of behaving. The insecurity can be expressed by people saying that they are not quite sure why they are there and they may not be able to contribute very much. There will be dependence on the person seen as the co-ordinator of the group. It is unlikely for disagreements to be discussed at this stage. People are wondering what the function of the group might be.

2. **Storming**

   Soon after this initial stage comes the element of competition and conflict. As the group works on defining the task and the way it will be accomplished, disagreements emerge. There may be challenges to the authority of the chair, or other significant people in the group. Some group members will stay silent and let others do the talking. There will be a sense of discomfort in the group.

3. **Norming**

   When the storming and power struggles are resolved, the group creates the ideas of what is normal and acceptable behaviour in this context. This will include language style. Group members begin to trust each other and exchange information in a more open way. Feelings can be shared, although there can be a fear that the group may still break up.

4. **Performing**

   Not all groups get to this stage. Those that do become very productive. The group members become genuinely collaborative in seeking to complete the assigned task. People trust each other and listen to other people's perspectives. The group tends to have high morale. Individuals feel good about membership of the group.

5. **Adjourning**

   At the end of the task, or life of the group, the members disengage and prepare for what is in effect, a small crisis: the end of the group. This can include a last minute panic or individuals displaying some distress about some aspect of the work they have or have not completed.

Let's look at an example of how these stages might be represented in a staff meeting.

The headteacher introduces the meeting:

> 'Today we are going to look at our approach to teaching sight words in Key Stage 1' The staff remain silent for a while (*forming*).

> Eventually a teacher starts to speak. 'Why do we need to do this? Is there a problem with the way that we have been working?' (*storming*).

> The head explains that it has been a long time since they had discussed the topic and an inspection is expected within the next two years.

> 'But we've always done it this way' says one of the teachers.

> 'And maybe that's the best way it can be done, but we ought to cover ourselves for the inspection. We don't want to find that we are criticised because our approach is seen to be outdated. What we are doing is generally effective, but let's make sure that there is not anything out there which we don't know about.' (leading to *norming*).

> 'Well we've used this particular programme and it still seems to be effective after five years.' Another teacher adds:

> 'We've been experimenting with this additional approach and it seems effective with some children with special needs, perhaps we could pool all the approaches in the school and see what we have got?' (*performing*).

Towards the end...

> 'Well there is so much to do here, we will never get it finished. Perhaps we should carry on in the next meeting.'

> The head reminds the group that the next meeting has already been allocated to another area.

> 'That's the problem with teaching, there is never enough time to do it properly.' (*adjourning*).

Think about the groups available in schools. They include staff meetings, Key Stage teams, groups who meet to agree programmes for specific children, review meetings and inspections. Next time you are part of one of these, look out for these stages. Can you identify the sequence?

Roles in teams

There are, however, other analyses of behaviour in groups. Belbin has considered the roles that people can take in work groups.

Belbin's nine team roles

Belbin analysed over 12,000 teams of adults and identified the different roles that people took. He suggested that the roles that people took were not necessarily reflections of personality, but more the kinds of functions required to make teams function effectively. His analytic method also offers a way of thinking about teams which are not performing. The analysis includes suggestions about tolerable weaknesses in people and the kinds of tasks that might be appropriate for them.

The roles are: co-ordinator, shaper, monitor/evaluator, resource investigator, team worker, implementer, completer finisher and specialist.

Let us consider each one:

Co-ordinators set the task, clarify the goals, summarise, delegate and utilise the strengths of the individual team members. They can sometimes be unpopular and can be considered to be manipulative and offload work to others. A good co-ordinator should be the chair or convener of the group.

Shapers take the role of directing the group towards its function. They work to overcome obstacles and try to ensure that the group has some shape or pattern to its work. They are good at reminding the group of the urgency of the task. On the other hand they can be somewhat provocative and not always sensitive to other people's feelings.

Plants are the unorthodox thinkers in the group. They offer unusual solutions to difficult problems, but can be too preoccupied to communicate well.

Resource investigators are optimistic, develop contacts and explore opportunities with people outside the group. They can be over optimistic and lose enthusiasm once the initial idea has passed, but can be very useful in creating links and resources for the project, provided they report back to the team. They are good at generating solutions to difficult problems.

Monitor evaluators look at all the options and judge them realistically. They ensure that the team does not fly off into irrational and unrealistic directions. They don't always inspire creativity, but do ensure that all the options have been considered.

Team workers support team members by building on their strengths and ideas. They foster good communications in the team and are good at playing a floating role in meetings. They are good at using diplomacy to resolve differences, however can be indecisive in difficult situations.

Implementers take the ideas and turn them into a practical and workable form. They carry out ideas once the team has decided what needs to be done. They are good at ensuring the ideas are carried out accurately, but are inclined to worry and don't always respond to new possibilities very easily.

Completer-finishers ensure that the project is completed on time and to the appropriate specification. They examine the small parts of the project which can get ignored. They ensure that the project is successful after the initial enthusiasm has passed. Although they are inclined to worry, they are vital for the successful completion of the task.

Specialists take the role of expert in the group. They feed information into the team and make sure that there is a professional view in the discussion. They tend to contribute on a rather narrow front, but are good at providing knowledge and techniques if they are in short supply.

Belbin's categories cover nine different roles, although there are many teams or groups which have fewer members. It is possible for one team member to take a number of different roles in the meeting. It is also possible for more than one person to occupy the same role, although this can lead to frustrations all round. As a teaching assistant you may find yourself able to take a variety of roles. Teams which do not work, or are not very productive, tend to lack the range of people required to fulfil the tasks described above. Think about the roles you have taken in teams. Teaching assistants are in a position to take a variety of roles. Are you more comfortable in some of the roles outlined above than in others? Can you see how groups can be made more successful and productive by thinking about the roles that we take? Can we vary our role to fill gaps in team roles?

Let us take an example of a group that is convened to write an individual education plan (IEP) for a disabled child, Shane who is joining the class.

Shane has Duchene Muscular Dystrophy, a muscle-wasting condition and is a powered wheelchair user. He will probably not live to see his twentieth birthday. He can get distressed and rude. He swears a lot and is not always very co-operative.

There are six people:

    The special needs coordinator (SENCo)
    The headteacher (HT)
    The class teacher (CT)
    The learning support assistant (LSA)
    The educational psychologist (EP)
    The parent (P)

HT [Co-ordinator] – Our aim here is to put together an IEP for Shane who is coming next month. We need to do this to justify our request for extra support. We all know that Shane is going to challenge our skills as educators. Could the EP outline the key points, perhaps.

EP [Shaper] – Well, Shane is going to need a physical management programme. You are going to need to look at basic care needs such as feeding, going to the toilet, and getting around the school safely. You are also going to need a plan for when Shane gets upset. His last teacher found this the most difficult part of having him in the class.

SENCo [Implementer] – This sounds like a tall order. OK. For the toileting, we can arrange for him to use the disabled loo near the school office. How often does he need to go?

P – He is OK if he can go at break and lunch times. Only if he is not very well does he need to go between times.

SENCo [Team worker] – So the LSA can take him at the beginning of break then.

P [Shaper] – But won't that mean that he misses out on the social side of break? Isn't it more important that he mixes with the other children? That's the side of school he likes most, yet finds most difficult. I would rather that he missed the end of the previous lesson than the social time at break.

CT [Monitor evaluator] – Well, that would mean that he misses the conclusion of the lesson. That's the time I summarise the main points, you know.

LSA [Team worker] – I'm sure that we can get round that one. After all, he won't be able to help much with the clearing away. I can take him then. And it means that I will get a bit of a break myself.

CT [Monitor evaluator] – But what if I set the homework at the end of the lesson, he won't know what to do?

HT [Resource investigator and co-ordinator] – Perhaps you can collect it from one of the other children or the LSA could liaise with the class teacher about the homework? I think these problems are addressable. Perhaps we should move on to look at the more complex matter of the temper outbursts?

CT [Monitor Evaluator] –Well I can't consider having him being rude in front of the others. If he wants to be included in the class, he has to follow the rules.

HT [Resource investigator] – Perhaps, Mrs X you could tell us what happens at home?

P – Well he does have his moments. If he has got one on him, there's not a lot you can do. I know I shouldn't, but I have unplugged his wheelchair when he has started to hit his sister with it. It can hurt quite a lot. I don't know what you can do in a classroom. He does get upset sometimes, but it's hardly surprising is it? He knows what is happening to him. When he went into the electric wheelchair he went very quiet and then it all came out. He was very difficult for several months. What you really need to do is just be nice with him and put up with it.

CT [Monitor evaluator] – Well I couldn't put up with that sort of thing. I have all the other children to consider.

SENCo [Shaper] –Perhaps what we should be looking at is a kind of plan so that we all do the same thing.

EP [Specialist] – That's a good idea. I have worked with similar situations elsewhere. What we might begin with is a set of principles? We know that he might get upset and that he might be rude when he is upset. So what we need is a way of teaching Shane how to manage his distress in a more acceptable way. You could start by re-stating some of the classroom rules about being polite and friendly to people. Make sure that he receives a lot of positive encouragement and praise when he is showing consideration for others. That way he may feel more accepted. And he may get very upset. Classrooms are really difficult places for anyone – teacher or pupil – to get angry. You might consider giving him permission to leave the classroom if he knows that he might lose his temper. You could give him a card which he leaves on his desk. He could then go to a pre-arranged place until he calms down. This way we can acknowledge that he has good reason to get upset, but that the class also has work to do.

CT [Monitor evaluator] – Well....., but what if he doesn't use the card?

EP [Specialist] – You still have the option of sending him out. As you say, you have a responsibility to the rest of the class.

SENCo [Team worker] – So is that what I will write on the IEP?

EP [Team worker] – That's really up to you. You have to feel that it is workable.

HT [Co-ordinator] – I think that's reasonable. So let me summarise. We will remind him of the polite and friendly rule and make sure that we praise him when he is following that rule. In addition, we will give him a card which allows him to leave the class if he knows that it is all too much for him. He can come to the office and calm down there. Is that OK with everyone?

CT – OK, I'll give it a go.

SENCo [Completer Finisher] – I'll prepare the card and write the IEP.

We have attempted to construct a fairly realistic meeting. Try to imagine the same meeting if everyone took the same or similar roles.

HT [Co-ordinator] – Our aim here is to put together an IEP for Shane who is coming next month. We need to do this to justify our request for extra support. We all know that Shane is going to challenge our skills as educators. Could the EP outline the key points, perhaps.

EP [Co-ordinator] – Exactly so, Headmaster. What we need is to create a plan which justifies the request. The plan must make sense to those people who make the decisions.

SENCo [Shaper] – I have the job of writing down the plan, so what do I write?

CT [Co-ordinator] – I am the one who will have to carry out the plan, so I need to know what I have to do.

HT [Co-ordinator] – The plan must meet the needs of our school. It must be practical and relevant.

EP [Co-ordinator] – The plan must also meet the needs of the child. That's what we mean by an individual education plan.

SENCo [Shaper] – I still have the job of writing down the plan, so what do I write?

CT [Co-ordinator] – I am still the one who will have to carry out the plan, so I need to know what I have to do.

The meeting continues to go round in circles and fails to achieve its goal through the lack of variety of roles played out in the group. The LSA could make a valuable contribution by adopting one (or more) of the missing roles.

References and further reading

Belbin, M. (1981) *Management Teams: They Succeed or Fail* Butterworth Heineman

Tuckman, B and Jensen, M (1977) 'Stages of Small Group Development' Group and *Organisational Studies* Vol 2 pp419-427

9

Groups, Attitudes and Prejudice

This chapter

- ■ describes the term 'attitude' as used in psychology

- ■ analyses the development of prejudice

- ■ considers ways of reducing negative attitudes towards minority groups

nevitably, groups of people who spend time together share experiences. These shared experiences lead to the development of shared knowledge, behaviour and attitudes. In this section we consider the implications of this, with particular emphasis on the development of prejudice and stereotypes, through the formation of attitudes.

In psychology, we use the term 'attitude' in a rather more limited sense than is found in popular conversation. T-shirts may have slogans such as *Boys with attitude*, but the sense used in psychology refers to preferences for evaluated items or events. In other words 'attitude' means our views about things, people or events. The evaluation includes elements of knowledge, emotion and behaviour.

For this to take place there are a number of mental processes involved. The first is *categorisation*. We must be able to define and recognise what we have an attitude to. If we consider attitudes towards minority groups, we must be able to recognise both the group and that each person is a member of this group. The second is *evaluation*. We must be able to identify whether some element is good or bad, better or worse than something else. The evaluation might be absolute, as in: all genocide is bad, or comparative, as in: murdering in cold blood is worse than killing someone in self-defence, but there is a need to be able to compare. The third is that it is based on *information*. Information, in this context covers *knowledge, emotion* and *behaviour.*

The importance of considering all three was demonstrated by a landmark study in the 1930s by LaPiere, an American psychologist who was examining racism. He was concerned with possible discrepancies between attitudes which were researched by looking at what people say and what they actually do in practice. At the time of the research there was no anti-discrimination legislation. In fact, racism was commonplace and accepted as normal. We might now consider the existence of white-only bars, buses and restaurants, along with apartheid systems of government, as being morally abhorrent, but these concepts were widely accepted until relatively recently.

LaPiere used a Chinese couple and watched them try to get served in over two hundred restaurants and hotels. He tried to watch from a distance to minimise any effects which his presence as a white American might have had. The Chinese couple were personable and charming. Their English was good and they were socially skilled. In spite of the prejudices of the time, they were accepted at all of the establishments except one. LaPiere followed up this experience with a questionnaire asking the proprietors whether they would accept Chinese guests. Over 120 returned the questionnaire of which 92 per cent indicated that they would not. In other words, people may say one thing and do something quite different. This particular study suggests that the people involved behaved in a much less racist way than they would have declared in the survey. There are a number of possible explanations. The couple were linguistically very competent and socially skilled, they were there in person. The Milgram study reported in chapter 8 demonstrates the importance of other people being in the same room. Those questioned may have had some suspicions of the motives behind the written questionnaire. What this study does demonstrate, however, are some of the difficulties surrounding the measurement of attitudes.

The most common tool for measuring attitudes is the use of a *Likert* scale. An example is:

Including children with physical difficulties is good for a school.				
1	2	3	4	5
Strongly agree	Agree	Neutral	Disagree	Strongly disagree

Subjects are invited to indicate the statement which most reflects their view. This method can be very useful when asking children about their attitudes to different aspects of their education. Prior to a review of the education of a child with special educational needs the pupil concerned can express their view through this diagrammatic method:

The teaching assistant draws the above line and says 'This is my *good* at and *bad* at line. I'm going to ask you to show me whether you are *good* at something or *bad* at it. If I say something that you are really *good* at, I want you to draw a line here, near to my *good* at box.'

'If I say something that you are really *bad* at, I want you to draw a line here, near to my *bad* at box.'

'Sometimes I might say something that you are neither *good* nor *bad* at. You are in the *middle*. If this is the case you put the line in the *middle*. Like this...'

'I might say something which you are quite *good* at, but not really good at. In this case, you put the line nearer the *good* at box, but not at the box. Like this....'

'And I might say something which you are a bit *bad* at, but not really *bad* at. In this case, you put the line nearer the *bad* at box, but not *at* the box. Like this....'

'The nearer you put the line to the *good* at box, the better you are at something, the nearer you put the line at the *bad* At box, the worse you are at it.'

This kind of technique can be used with more pairs of terms than good/bad. Examples include like/dislike, friendly/unfriendly. It can also be used to enable children to indicate their attitudes to themselves. You can ask children to show where they are on the line at the moment and where they would like to be in six month's time. The difference between the two gives an indication of the degree of satisfaction in the child. Consider the following example of a child asked about his/her reading abilities:

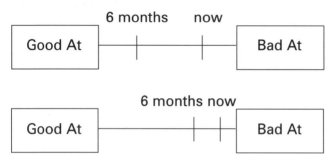

We would infer that the child who indicated the first line was wanting to change their reading. The second child wants change much less.

The use of these kinds of techniques with individuals is quite common; their use with large groups of subjects is more problematic. In fact, even if you ensure that you only use studies that ensure a match between behaviour and reported attitude the usefulness of measuring attitudes to predict future behaviour can be quite limited. This has not prevented a whole industry to being set up in which researchers survey public attitudes on a wide range of subjects. What is more useful, however, is the application of this kind of research into understanding the ways in which minority groups are represented and, through that, a better understanding of the nature of prejudice and racism.

If we take the social constructionist's view that knowledge is not *out there*, but constructed by interactions between people, we can look at the way in which objects and people are represented in day-to-day situations. If we go to a super-market to buy food, the food packaging illustrates the content. The low fat spread I buy is made in a large factory, but the picture suggests that is comes from a countryside with olive groves. Cars advertising features countryside rather than the more usual city. A CNN broadcast in February 2004 represented the detainees in Guantanamo Bay as being glad to be in a US prison because the conditions were so good there. These examples all create a *social representation* of food, cars and American prisons. These social representations not only provide methods of communication, but ways of discriminating between social groups and objects.

> **Exercise**: Take two or three different newspapers and look at the ways in which children are represented. Look at the language used to describe them. Look at the actions that are reported. Write a list of the positive and negative features. Which is longer. What impression do the papers create of children? How might this affect people's attitudes to children?

Representations are not only found on paper. The language used in conversations are representations of objects, actions and people. Sensitivity to the use of language is greater than thirty years ago. Many terms used to describe minority groups, such as ethnic, sexual orientation and disabled are now considered unacceptable. We will consider the use of psychology to the issues of prejudice and racism.

Psychology of discrimination

Discrimination is expressed in very practical ways. In the UK there are at least four dimensions:

- violent physical attacks against minority groups
- public opinion and hostility towards difference
- economic inequalities between groups
- educational performance

In order for these events to occur, certain processes must take place. The two most important ones are:

- separation of self from 'other'
- establishment of stereotypes

Separation

When we think about different groups we focus on those elements which emphasise their differences such as skin colour, religious practices etc. However, for racist and discriminatory practices to emerge, there must be a separation of the ways in which we see ourselves from the ways we see others. *They* are not like *us* because *they* do different things from us. So we see others as different from us. Ironically, the greater understanding we have of DNA suggests that there are greater differences within racial groups than between them. Eighty-five per cent of the genetic differences between us are found within individuals in the same group: only 7 per cent are found between the major racial groups. No genetic variation has yet been found associated with sexual orientation.

Separation of ourselves from others has been the subject of some important psychological research. The example here is the Sherif and Sherif *summer camp* experiments.

In the US, there is a tradition of summer camp for school-aged children. In this study, children were chosen for their ordinariness and mainstream backgrounds. The children did not know each other before arriving at the camp. On arrival, the usual process of forming friends occurred. The experimenters carefully watched the patterns emerging and children were able to choose their roommates.

Experiment 1. Establishment of different groups. The experimenters divided the children into two groups, taking care to separate children who were becoming friendly with each other. The groups were given names and activities to do together. As expected, the different groups shared codes, secret places and norms of behaviour. The new friendships were within the new groups, rather than reflections of previous ones.

Experiment 2. Competition between groups. The organisers arranged tournaments and situations in which only one of the two groups could win. The points were arranged so that the groups were close together. The groups began to show some elements of hostility. They called each other names, glorified their own achievements and disparaged those of the other team. There was a strong sense of in-group and out-group membership. If you were in the same team, you were *in*, if not, you were *out*. The children were very positive towards the in-group and very hostile towards the out-group.

Experiment 3. Co-operation between groups. In the final stage, the organisers arranged activities which involved the groups co-operating in solving problems such as a broken-down car and tasks which could only be achieved by both groups working together. They also introduced a third group of children. To a degree this provided a 'common enemy'. The social situation returned to something like that found at the beginning of the stay.

This study is widely reported. Follow-up studies have tended to confirm its findings. It underlines the influence that separating the self from others can have on human behaviour. It gives us insight into the first process associated with discrimination and prejudice.

Stereotypes

When we create stereotypes, we link attributes to particular items. For example 'all cheap biscuits taste horrible' or 'all daytime television is boring' might reflect the beliefs of some people. Such statements imply some evaluation: it may be good or bad, but if those beliefs are held, they generalise to other items in the set. So if a new manufacturer produced a type of biscuit and sold it at a cheap price, people who held the prejudice that cheap equals horrible may assume that the new biscuit range could not possibly taste nice because of their previously held prejudice. Similarly, the arrival of a new TV programme during the day may be viewed negatively because of the prejudice about daytime TV.

You can see the link with the ideas of categorising as a mental process that allows us to make sense of complex situations. However, our mental processes go further than this, as an influential experiment demonstrated.

Tajfel and Wilkes created a simple method. They presented subjects with eight lines presented in different ways. They were arranged in two groups of four.

Condition 1

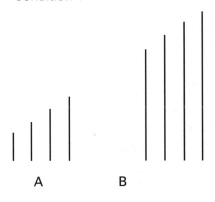

Condition 2

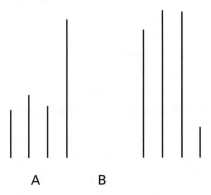

Condition 3

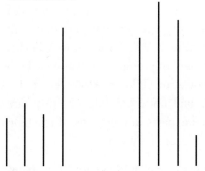

The subjects were then asked to judge the lengths of the lines in the two groups. As you can see, the lines in condition one were arranged so that all of the shorter ones were in one group and all of the longer ones in the other. In condition 2 they were arranged randomly, but given group names A and B. In condition 3 they were arranged in the same random order, but not given group names. The results were surprising.

In condition 1, subjects exaggerated the differences between the two groups. They were able to form a stereotype for the two groups. Group A has shorter lines than group B. They also exaggerated the similarity of the lines within the groups. In other words they tended to over-estimate the similarities of the lines in group A, thus exaggerating the differences between the groups.

In condition 2, subjects exaggerated the similarities between the lines in groups A and B when compared with condition 3. Remember that the arrangement of lines was the same in both conditions. In other words, the presence of a *label* (A or B) created the conditions for the subjects to alter the way they saw the lines. So, the generation of stereotypes is easy and depends on both *differences* and *labels*.

Fairly neutral examples have deliberately been used so far to illustrate these processes, but the application of these principles to human conditions means tackling the phenomenon of prejudice. Prejudice is the result of separation and stereotype. If we see ourselves as different from a different group of people and are able to generate a stereotype, we can create prejudice. Groups of people who have differences in belief, skin colour, sexual practices or physical abilities can all be the subject of human prejudice. These processes have serious implications for teaching assistants working in schools.

The trend in education has been towards *including* children from all backgrounds and, increasingly, children with special needs. It is now time to look at the role of education in reducing prejudice towards minority groups.

The 1944 Education Act introduced the idea of *categories* of children with different educational needs. This led to the development of different categories of schools. Children were assessed and allocated a category. They were then sent to a school which was appropriate to that category. We can see now that this created the perfect conditions for the development of prejudice. It was easy both to separate and stereotype these different groups of children. However, it also allowed for conditions in which knowledge and understanding of fairly rare childhood conditions grew. Educators became experts in the fields of teaching children who previously had not been in the education system at all.

The trend towards social and educational inclusion sets out to change this. Now, children are not categorised but seen as having different educational needs. This has necessitated a change in the way we see children with differences. Historically, we have adopted a *Medical Model* of disability. This can be visualised as in the diagram below:

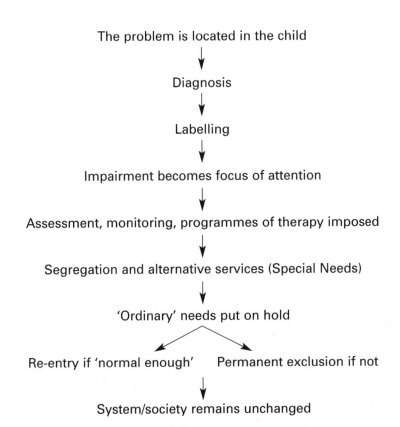

MEDICAL MODEL

The problem is located in the child

↓

Diagnosis

↓

Labelling

↓

Impairment becomes focus of attention

↓

Assessment, monitoring, programmes of therapy imposed

↓

Segregation and alternative services (Special Needs)

↓

'Ordinary' needs put on hold

Re-entry if 'normal enough'   Permanent exclusion if not

↓

System/society remains unchanged

As you can see, the conditions for prejudice are well established. Both separation and stereotype development are possible. The child is seen to have the problem. When/if the child is *fixed* then the child can return to society. Whilst this way of thinking may work well for hospitals, there are many differences in people that will not change.

An alternative is the *Social Care Model* of disability. This is visualised like this:

SOCIAL MODEL

The problem is within the interactions between the world and the child

↓

Strengths and needs defined by self and others

↓

Outcome – programmes are designed

↓

Resources made available to family/school

↓

Training for parents and professionals

↓

Relationships nurtured

↓

Diversity welcomed

↓

System/society evolves

Rather than seeing children as having things wrong with them, we focus on the way children interact with the world. Children may need assistance. A child using a wheelchair needs ramps and wide, self opening doors. A child called *hyperactive* may need opportunities to be more active than other children: children who learn more slowly may need their learning tasks to be broken down into smaller chunks. In other words we focus on children's needs in terms of accessing the school curriculum – which may need substantial modification – rather than trying to fix the child. This reduces the opportunities for separation and stereotyping and thus the conditions required for prejudice to develop. However, there is another social advantage: identification.

Identification

The counterpart of prejudice is identification. If prejudice involves separation, identification involves perceiving similarity. People will identify with some groups and not others. Identification includes attitudes, opinions and beliefs which are considered to be held in common. For adults involved with children this is particularly important to understand. The first group with whom the child will relate is the social group in which they are raised – usually a family. However, this is neither the sole nor the most attractive group that children are exposed to. Children will find different groups at school and in depictions in popular media. The group children relate to most will have a large influence on their attitudes and behaviour.

An experimental study of this process was carried out by Kelly and Woodruff back in 1956. Their subjects were students at a college which prided itself on its progressive teaching methods. The students were played a sound recording of a speech calling for a return to more traditional methods of tuition. At regular intervals, the speech was interrupted by applause. One half of the students were told that the audience were members of the general public, the other half were told that they were students from the college. The students who believed that the applause came from the public did not change their views about tuition methods, whereas those who believed that it came from other students did change their views towards those suggested in the speech. They concluded that the students were influenced, not by the applause, but by the belief that those applauding were like themselves. In psychology we call these *reference* groups. These have been defined as:

> ...groups to which the individual relates their self as a part or to which they aspires to relate their self psychologically.

They are particularly important in the formation of attitudes. When there is conflict between the attitudes of parents and peers, adolescents are more likely to adopt the attitude of their peers rather than parents. For children, there are many sources of possible reference groups. Characters in TV shows, images used by advertisers, as well as those found in schools can all suffice. Is this a hopeless situation? Is it possible for adults to influence the attitudes of children at all or are they simply listening to the views of others of their own age? An interesting insight was established over fifty years ago. Experimenters were concerned with the ways in which attitudes to food could change. In one condition, people were given a forty-five minute lecture about the benefits of eating particular foods. The vitamin and mineral values of the foods were explained and the health benefits stressed. In the other condition, a group discussion was held about ways to tackle the problems of unhealthy eating. In both conditions, only forty-five minutes was allowed for the message to be communicated. The experimenters looked at the subsequent food purchases of each group. Of those informed via the lecture method, only 3 per cent had changed their buying of more healthy foods. This compared to 32 per cent for the discussion group. These changes in purchasing remained stable over a long period of time. In schools a similar picture emerges. If we wish to increase tolerance of difference and diversity, a discussion, not a lecture is most effective. Messages from heroes and pop stars are likely to be heeded more than those from teachers and assistants.

References and further reading

Hilgard, E (1996) *Hilgard's Introduction to Psychology* London Harcourt Brace
Whetherell, M (ed) (1996) *Identities, Groups and Social Issues* London Sage

10

The Psychology of Conflict and Aggression

This chapter

- describes the phenomenon of aggression from different psychological perspectives
- examines bullying and ways of reducing it in school

As with many other areas of human behaviour and experience, there are a number of different ways of looking at these issues. We begin with the biology of aggression.

Anger and aggression are associated with the production of *adrenalin*. When released into our bloodstream, our bodies suddenly become capable of exerting greater strength or performing faster. This is known as the 'flight or fight' response. We are able to run faster or fight harder. There are other physiological processes associated with this. Energy is needed, so the liver releases extra sugar, heart rate and blood pressure rise. Less essential mechanisms shut down, so saliva and mucus dry up. Natural pain killers called *endorphins* are secreted. More red blood vessels are released so that more oxygen can be carried to the muscles.

However, the conditions in which these changes to the body occur are primarily social and depend on the perception of a threat. In addition, the ways in which we respond to these chemical changes in our bodies are subject to other factors. This was explored by an important experiment carried out by Schacter and Singer. Subjects were given an injection of epinephine (the chemical associated with the release of adrenalin). Some subjects were told that the chemical would induce a state of euphoria (light-headedness) and others were told that it would make them feel angry. Each subject was left in a waiting room after they had been told of the side effects of the injection. Also in the waiting room was another person. In fact, this was an actor. If the subject had been told that the chemical would induce euphoria, the actor behaved in a euphoric way. The actors acted angrily with those who were told they would feel angry. The real subjects were asked to report on the side-effects. As you might expect, the subjects were influenced by the behaviour of the actors. Those told about anger and faced with an act of anger reported that they experienced anger. Similar responses were found for the euphoric situations. So we conclude that even in situations with a well understood biological mechanism, there are mental processes which influence our responses. Anger may be a primary emotion, but the way in which it is expressed is socially defined. Children can be taught to manage anger and express it in socially acceptable ways.

Anger and aggression appear to be universal. Therefore, we might reasonably suppose that they have an important function which will help the individual survive and have children. Two complementary functions are possible for anger and aggression.

The first is *defence*. If a child is being threatened, anger and aggression are ways to survive. The adrenalin enables the individual fight harder or run faster. The triggers for this mechanism might not be obvious. If children perceive that somebody else is gaining an advantage, this could be seen as a threat. Fairness is very important for children – as it is for adults.

The second is *display*. Children, particularly adolescents, may use displays of anger and aggression to achieve a higher status. This high status may have the advantage of making them more attractive to potential partners. A child is more likely to display anger if there is an audience, particularly if that audience has either other members of the same sex, who might compete for partners, or if there are potential partners in the audience who might be impressed by the display. In both cases, anger is likely to be useful to the individual. For the adults in school, getting the child away from the audience, or the audience away from the child is a high priority. Removal of the child can raise their status in the eyes of some.

There are other unexpected implications for adults working with children, whether as teachers or assistants. The level of arousal associated with the situation of anger and aggression can be very high and therefore exciting. Once a child has experienced this, they might learn to generate situations in which this is repeated. Children who are restrained when angry or aggressive may find this restraint exciting and rewarding. If so, they may behave in ways that repeat the event.

The variations in culture of children and their families produce variations in the way children express their feelings. This has been explored by psychologists using methods from *social constructionism*. When adults talk with young children, they will describe the expression of anger through stories. In one study, Miller and Sperry (1987) the stories were analysed and two key ideas were found. They were *sissy* and *spoiled*. The messages that were given to children were:

- there are times in life when you face anger and aggression. You must stand up for yourself

- even young children from two years need to understand this

- when we talk about anger and aggression, we tend to describe what we did rather than what we felt

When the analysis was taken further, the themes became:

- if another child hurts you, defend yourself (don't be a sissy)

- don't be aggressive without reason (don't be spoiled)

- if your mother teases you, show that you can stand up for yourself (don't be sissy)

- don't direct anger at grown ups (don't be spoiled)

For children starting school, different families will give different messages. Children will need to be introduced to ways of responding to aggression through discussion. Distinctions may need to be made. New rules apply. The school's message is likely to be that when children are in school, they need to tell a teacher if someone is hurting them or somebody else. This may be different from the way children deal with such situations at home. It may be necessary to discuss the idea that there can be other ways of responding to anger. The ways children respond in school may need to differ from those adopted at home, in the street or on the football terraces.

For psychoanalysts, aggression represents a fundamental human drive. By and large, we are unaware of our fundamental motivations, because they are unconscious. We are driven towards a particular goal. If the path to this goal is blocked, we get frustrated and angry. Anger has energy and if that energy is not released, it stays in our system and is released in other ways. Anger can build up until it is finally expressed in some outlet. If we do not release our anger, it can have a damaging effect on the individual. Our expression of anger is held in check by our inhibitions. When people find themselves in groups, inhibitions are removed and it is easier to express anger. Crowds can become very aggressive. The violence associated with football crowds is actually quite healthy as it allows the release of pent-up aggression. Crowds actually allow the individual to be more instinctive. In school, our task is to teach the child to recognise anger and to find acceptable ways of expressing it. Group activities such as competitive sports do not create anger, but situations in which it can be released. However, these views are by no means socially accepted. There is a strong view from other schools of psychology that active competitive sports function to create the conditions for anger to be aroused. One such challenge comes from social learning theory.

Social learning theory emphasises the way in which we learn by watching others. The term *modelling* is used to describe this kind of learning. The supporters of this theory suggest that aggression can be learned through imitation. This idea was tested in a nursery. Young children were shown an adult behaving in a violent and aggressive way towards a blown-up doll. When the children were left to play with the doll, they too behaved in a violent and aggressive way. Even more disturbing was the finding that children who watched a film of an adult or a cartoon character behaving aggressively were likely to act in the same way. This study led to many others looking at the influence of aggression on TV. Large-scale studies have generally agreed that watching violence on TV leads to increases in interpersonal aggression.

This information has some important implications for teachers and teaching assistants. If we accept that observations of others resolving conflict in a violent and aggressive way, are important sources of learning for children, then we must also accept that it is possible for adults to demonstrate socially acceptable ways of resolving conflict.

Bullying

Perhaps the most common display of aggression in schools is found in bullying. Before we consider the psychology, let us examine the phenomenon. Olweus defined bullying in 1992 in the following way:

> A student is being bullied or victimised when he or she is exposed, repeatedly over time, to negative actions on the part of one or more other students. (Olweus, 1992)

The behaviours associated with bullying are many:

- verbal bullying includes threatening, teasing, taunting and name-calling

- physical bullying includes hitting, punching, pinching, pushing and stealing valued items (eg packed lunches)

- emotional bulling includes making faces, excluding someone from a group and refusing to comply with other people's wishes

Bullying can be carried out by a single person or a group. Likewise, the target of bullying can be a single person or a group. Those involved in bullying can take the roles of bully, victim, bully/victim or bystander.

The facts around bullying are stark. A national survey in Norway revealed that about 15 per cent of students were involved in bullying. Nine per cent were victims, 7 per cent were bullies and 1.6 per cent were both bullies and victims. A British survey in Cleveland suggested that about 25 per cent of students were involved in bullying, 10 per cent were bullies, 7 per cent were victims and 6 per cent were bully/victims. The survey also revealed gender differences: boys were more likely to use physical methods whilst girls were more likely to use verbal and emotional methods.

Within the bully population there are categories:

The majority are *aggressive bullies*: Typically these

- are aggressive to all people, irrespective of authority
- show poor impulse control
- see violence positively
- like to dominate
- are physically and emotionally strong
- have high self esteem
- are insensitive to others

About 20 per cent of bullies are *anxious bullies*. They

- are anxious and aggressive
- have low self esteem
- are insecure and do not have friends
- pick on stronger students than they are
- provoke attacks by more powerful students
- are emotionally unstable

The third group are *passive bullies*. They

- are easily dominated
- passive and easily led
- are not particularly aggressive
- have empathy for others
- feel guilty after acts of bulling

The consequences of being bullied are many:

- fear of attending school
- deterioration of school work
- having school clothes, books or work torn or destroyed

- coming home hungry (because dinner money/packed lunch has been stolen)
- becoming withdrawn
- stammering
- acting out aggressively with other children
- eating disorders
- attempted or actual suicide
- crying themselves to sleep
- bed wetting
- nightmares
- unexplained bruises, scratches and cuts
- stealing money (to pay the bully)
- refusal to say what is wrong
- giving improbable explanations for any of the above actions

Studies also reveal that some common hypotheses about bullying are not, in fact, true. The reality is that

- girls are just as likely to be the victims of bullying as boys, although boys are more likely to bully than girls

- bullying is just as likely to occur in a small school in a rural area as in big schools in an inner city area. In fact the staff in the inner city area are more likely to be aware of bullying as an issue than staff in the rural school and to have policies and strategies for dealing with it

- bullying is just as likely in schools with small class sizes as large

- bullying is not an inevitable part of children growing up. There are things you can do about it. If you stop it in one place it does not emerge somewhere else

- children from minority groups are no more likely to be victims than children from majority groups. There is, however, a greater likelihood that children who are physically less strong will be victims of bullying. Similarly, children, particularly boys, who bully are likely to be physically stronger than average

Psychology can make a contribution to tackling bullying in schools. There is a biological dimension. Bullying is not simply a human problem. Behaviour similar to bullying has been observed in animals. The term *mobbing* has been used to describe behaviour in chimpanzees, baboons and a large variety of birds, such as tits, blackbirds and even humming birds. Large groups of animals or birds will attack a perceived threat. Small birds will attack an owl. There are two benefits for the small birds. First, the owl is a predator. As individuals they are unable to defend against this threat, but as a group, they can. Secondly, there is an opportunity to learn more about the threat. The small birds are curious. Baboons will mob tigers, ground squirrels will mob snakes, and chimpanzees will mob a leopard. One observer noted that the way the chimpanzees attacked the leopard was by ganging up, rushing, screaming, stamping their feet and throwing objects at it. Eventually, one of the chimps attacked the animal with a stick. The observer drew parallels with the way humans have treated wild animals, suggesting that our behaviour is closer to that of apes than we might find comfortable. With humans, we cannot ignore the differences between genders. Although girls are just as likely to be victims, boys are more likely to be perpetrators. The biological dimension suggests that there may be an advantage in bullying: the individual may stand a greater chance of attracting a mate in a competitive environment.

The social constructionist dimension adds different information. Children do not want to admit that they are being bullied. There is a degree of shame. Some elements of our culture discourage them from discussing this with other children or adults. One eleven-year old girl said:

> I think I felt that I was the only person that had ever been bullied and if I told anybody they would think that I was stupid and a wimp. (Reported in Elliott, 1992)

Even if you do discuss this with an adult, the response is not always helpful. One fourteen-year old girl said:

> When a friend told the teacher I was being bullied he said I was old enough to deal with it myself. (Reported in Elliott, 1992)

Admitting that you are the victim involves reshaping the way that you present yourself to other people. Keeping quiet allows the victim to present a different, more successful image to others close to them.

Learning theory adds yet more information. For the bully, there is something to be gained by his or her acts. Bullying is rewarded by the admiration, or fear, of others. Status can rise. For the victim, putting up with the acts of the bully may be less humiliating than talking about it to others. Social learning theory suggests that bullies may learn how to bully by watching others. If staff in school use physical or emotional strength to get their own way, the message conveyed is that bullying is an acceptable way of getting people to do what you want. Although physical attack is illegal, adults in school can use language to humiliate children and each other. Sarcasm is one such outlet. If we consider that bullying involves a set of learned behaviours, we suggest that the bully may not have the necessary social skills to get admiration in other ways.

Psychodynamic psychology suggests that there are fears in the mind of the bully. A child who is in some way different reminds the bully of some insecurity of their own. The act of bullying protects the bully from ideas that they are like the victim. In the mind of the bully, bullying makes them a better person because they reject or repress the part of themselves that they do not like. A strong bully attacks a weak victim because they are frightened to admit that there is a part of the victim that reminds them of part of themselves.

These ideas point to ways of reducing bullying. There are a number of different approaches and strategies. The first is to create a culture in which children can talk without shame about being bullied. Anonymous reporting, the use of drama and visible school policies can help here. The second is to ensure that the discussion of feelings is an acceptable part of school life; that it is not shameful to say that you are unhappy. The third is to ensure that bullies are not rewarded for their actions. When found out, restitution can include public or private apologies face-to-face or in writing, along with presenting a special gift to the victim. For the bully who is insecure, personal counselling or inclusion in some social skills group may help. In addition, there are practical elements in both the design of the school and the ways in which areas are supervised. Bullying is unlikely to happen when adults are around. Areas of the school which are never supervised are breeding grounds for bullying.

Teaching assistants are in a particularly useful position in school to look for signs of bullying. They may have a closer relationship with individual students than the teachers do. Students may feel safer with their learning support assistant than with their teacher, so it would be good for the TAs to take a strong role in discussion groups and role plays.

Summary

Our aim in this chapter is to consider the research into the behaviour of people in groups and to apply the ideas relevant to the work of teaching assistants. As a teaching assistant you will probably have the opportunity to work in different groups. You will be able to take different roles to ensure that the tasks are completed. We hope the information you now have enables you to understand more about how groups work.

References and further reading

Elliot, M (1992) *Bullying – A Practical Guide to Coping in Schools* London Longman

Olweus, D (1993) *Bullying at School* Oxford Blackwell.

Wetherell, M (ed) (1996) *Identities, Groups and Social Issues* London Sage

Part 5
Trends and Future Developments

11

An International Perspective

This chapter

- considers changes to the role of a teaching assistant over time

- compares the current UK system of inclusive education with that found in Italy

T he current interest in the role of teaching assistants is welcome. There are increasing opportunities for teaching assistants to undertake bespoke training to degree level. We can only speculate what the future holds, but psychology suggests methods that might offer some ideas about the nature of the work over the next five or ten years. The methods involve looking at what has changed and what has remained constant in the past. Consider the following ideas.

It is over twenty years since the 1981 Education Act came in force. This legislation introduced the idea of integrating children with special education needs into mainstream schools. If we consider the role of teaching assistants working before that time with those working now, we can extract the elements of the job which have changed from those which are unchanged. There is also another source of information to assist in our speculations.

The Warnock Report was published in 1977. This report led to the 1981 Education Act and its principles of integration. The UK was not the only country to examine its approach to children with special needs. Italy saw a kind of cultural revolution in this area in the late 1960s. A similar system of segregated special education was in place, but a large number of professional parents who had children with some disability removed these children and enrolled them into local schools. In 1971 the law was changed and disabled children aged between six and fourteen were granted the *right* to a place in the local school. By 1977 the law required local schools to educate such children and all the special schools were closed. In 1987 the law was extended to require secondary schools to offer education up to nineteen and in 1992 this extended to universities. Not only are all children included in the local schools, but no alternatives exist.

The Italian system has many similarities with the UK. A disabled child has a right to an individual programme of education with individualised targets. A special needs support teacher works as part of a team, which may include a speech therapist, occupational or physiotherapist, educational psychologist and an ancillary assistant. Additionally, there may be an *assistenza sociale* or social assistant, employed by the Health Authority. This role is, perhaps, closer to that of a district nurse. The social assistant has a wider community-based role. The availability of this service to schools, on a regular basis, depends on the area, but some hold a kind of surgery in schools for children with disabilities.

Of course, there are some differences too. The main responsibility for teaching rests with the class teacher. The maximum class size is normally 31, although classes are normally smaller than this, typically 25-28. If a class has a child with a declared special need, the maximum size is reduced to twenty, but the group number is usually around fifteen. There can only be one disabled child in each class, unless there are special circumstances or the special need is considered not to be severe. There would not be a teaching assistant assigned specifically to sit and work with the child with special needs. The specialist teacher works directly with an individual for about six hours per week. These teachers have specialist qualifications and there is roughly one special needs teacher to every 138 pupils attending school. So there is approximately one special needs teacher to every two pupils considered to have a special need. In Italy, physical, sensory and cognitive needs are all considered to be disabilities.

Nationally, the number of children considered to be disabled is 1.56 per cent of the whole school population. This is less than in the UK system, but the majority of these children would probably be in some kind of special provision in the UK. If the UK is to continue the drive to include all children into the mainstream school system, Italy offers a model and a source of experience which has been in operation for nearly a generation.

We have interviewed teaching assistants working in education twenty plus years ago, alongside those working now. Additionally, we have interviewed special needs support staff in Italy. The questions of interest are:

■ what has changed?
■ what has stayed the same?

The study does not purport to be definitive, nor particularly rigorous, but it may provide information about future trends.

We will begin with the assistant working twenty plus years ago.

Highest qualification: O levels. She had been an auxiliary nurse before having her own children. She went to work in a residential school for disabled children as a physiotherapy aide. Unfortunately, a back injury led to her being unable to continue in this role. She then provided support to a severely physically disabled boy in the same school.

She described the range of activities as:

- 'translating' his communication by head movements for the class teacher
- feeding
- transferring him from one place to another
- assisting with his toileting
- setting up his computer equipment
- doing physiotherapy exercises with him
- following his instructions for experiments in science etc
- personal help (dressing etc)
- assisting in games and PE
- reading and writing for him, when necessary

The qualities needed were:

- empathy
- patience
- a good sense of humour
- physical and mental strength
- being able to think on your feet – lateral thinking
- some knowledge of disabilities
- keen eyes for reporting changes in a child's physical or mental state

She particularly enjoyed:

- the child's sense of humour
- understanding the child's wishes, he could say what he wanted, but only through me
- helping him to learn
- enabling him to take part in as many 'normal' activities as possible
- inventing gadgets to make his life better

If she had been able to change three things they would have been:

- getting more help lifting him
- reducing the hours of work (they were very long)
- increasing the personal freedom (or privacy) for children

This assistant went on to support two teenage girls in a comprehensive school before taking a position as a teaching assistant in a school for children with moderate learning difficulties. She retired in 2002. She added, at the end of the interview, that the job had become more like a secretary to a teacher, rather than working with individual students, although she did say that she was given more responsibility and had run a lunchtime gardening club at the school.

Two assistants in their twenties were interviewed in a similar way. Both were undertaking additional qualifications, with the aim of becoming qualified teachers. The first described her career path to date. She helped with reading at the school as a volunteer. She was first employed for eighteen hours per week, to support a child with *cerebral palsy*. After a year she spent four years working 25 hours per week before being offered a full-time contract. She was recently appointed as a learning mentor.

She described the range of activities undertaken and her varied roles:

- first-aider
- support dance teacher after school
- learning mentor
- swimming teacher
- support for fine motor programmes from the occupational therapist
- working in a nursery for nine months
- offering speech and language programmes for a range of children
- individual learning programmes on computers
- supporting children on school trips
- taking class lessons to cover teachers
- helping with planning lessons
- helping with annual reviews
- attending staff meetings and training sessions
- helping to toilet-train children
- taking a gross motor group
- supporting at lunchtime
- changing children's clothes
- offering emotional support

The qualities needed were:

- patience
- a good understanding of child development
- willingness for hard work
- ability to communicate well with other people
- to be kind and caring

She particularly enjoyed:

- taking the fine and gross motor groups
- art lessons
- handwriting lessons
- taking the speech and language groups

If there were things she would like to change, they would be:

- to be paid more
- to be recognised for what you do (we are not recognised enough)
- to have our qualifications taken into account when we go for further training

The second added the following to the above list of activities:

- assembling classroom displays
- dealing with rewards and sanctions
- behaviour tracking and observations of individual students
- preparing resources
- assisting in assembly by monitoring behaviour
- running the tuckshop
- reading stories

She also emphasised the following qualities:

- patience
- tolerance
- a fair attitude
- honesty
- a good role model
- enthusiasm

Her issues for improvement were:

- pay
- communication
- advance notice when required to do preparation

Before we move on to the Italian position, we highlight the similarities and differences between the positions twenty plus years ago and now.

Similarities

- a whole range of jobs are undertaken by teaching assistants. They do not do the same job for all of their careers

- they find themselves in a classroom with children and a teacher

■ they undertake teaching-like activities under the direction of a range of professionals

■ they help children with personal matters such as toileting and dressing

■ the need for empathy, patience and a sense of humour seems to transcend time, as do the aspirations for more help and recognition

Differences

■ qualifications are now available

■ there is a perception of career development: the possibility of becoming a teacher is part of the thinking of today's teaching assistants

■ there is more delegation of responsibility to today's teaching assistant

■ they are taking groups under the direction of other professionals

■ they are even taking whole classes when the teacher is unavailable.

Not mentioned above is development of a higher status known as Higher Level Teaching Assistant, which is set to create a new type of teaching assistant with a higher salary, in return for additional responsibilities.

The Italian system

There is no exact equivalent to a teaching or learning support assistant in Italy. Within a classroom, children who need help with writing may receive it from a variety of sources. The support teacher undertakes a role in delivering differentiated teaching, mainly in Italian and Maths. Children who need assistance in, for example, toileting, may call on the help of an auxiliary.

An auxiliary has no formal qualifications and duties include:

■ cleaning the school
■ opening and closing the building
■ going to the Post Office
■ contacting the school secretary
■ performing support services for teachers such as photocopying
■ assisting with handicapped pupils on trips and in the toilet

The lack of intervention in a classroom is a significant difference from the UK system is. Any curriculum-related activity comes from the support teacher. The support teacher *may* offer a child help in toileting, but this is entirely discretionary and many choose not to provide this service, leaving it to the auxiliary. At meal times a child requiring help may receive it from the class teacher, or other children. Pupils are considered to be a legitimate source of help for a child with special needs.

The qualities needed by the auxiliaries and support teachers include many of those outlined above. They include:

- knowledge of disabling conditions
- patience
- kindness
- flexibility
- ability to listen to childrens' worries

It must be said that the Italians interviewed were not particularly happy with the system. There were suggestions that closure of the special schools had been rushed and that proper provision in mainstream schools was not in place. The quality of teaching received from the mainstream class teacher by a child with special needs was very variable. That said, no one suggested that a system of segregated special schools should be re-introduced. New services are becoming available from agencies, like psychological support services. These services include training for teachers, parents, relatives and others. Team building, counselling skills and acceptance of diversity are among the titles of other courses on offer.

The future?

If we look at how the Italian system has evolved, it seems clear that some activities remain central and essential. There are needs to help children with basic tasks such as toileting, feeding and assistance on school trips. There are needs for differentiated teaching activities including the development of individualised education plans. There are needs to draw on the knowledge and skills of a range of professionals to assist in promoting the development of children with diversities. In the UK, there is a trend to increase the knowledge and skill-base of teaching assistants. If this is a successful initiative we could conceive of a future in which certain tasks are allocated to more skilled and qualified personnel. They may have more status, title and pay. However, there will always be the need for assistance with tasks that prime care-givers normally perform with younger children: toileting, feeding and mobility. We suspect that despite the developments in technology, these will continue to be the province of assistants.

This book has examined different aspects of the work of teaching assistants seen through the discipline of psychology. Inevitably, aspects have been omitted. We hope that the book constitutes a positive contribution to the lives and work of the teaching assistants working in schools at this time. As far as we can see, the future for teaching assistants has never looked so interesting.

Index